WRITING INSTRUCTION FOR ENGLISH LEARNERS

A Focus on Genre

D0493413

Eugenia Mora-Flores

CORWIN PRESS
A SAGE Company

For information:

Corwin Press
A SAGE Company
2455 Teller Road
Thousand Oaks, California 91320
www.corwinpress.com

SAGE Ltd.
1 Oliver's Yard
55 City Road
London, EC1Y 1SP
United Kingdom

SAGE Pvt. Ltd.
B 1/I 1 Mohan Cooperative
  Industrial Area
Mathura Road, New Delhi 110 044
India

SAGE Asia-Pacific Pte. Ltd.
33 Pekin Street #02-01
Far East Square
Singapore 048763

Printed in the United States of America

Library of Congress Cataloging-in-Publication Data

Mora-Flores, Eugenia, 1975-
Writing instruction for English learners: a focus on genre/Eugenia Mora-Flores.
    p. cm.
Includes bibliographical references and index.
ISBN 978-1-4129-5728-1 (cloth)
ISBN 978-1-4129-5729-8 (pbk.)
  1. English language—Composition and exercises—Study and teaching—Foreign speakers.
2. English language—Study and teaching—Foreign speakers. I. Title.

PE1404.M665 2009
808'.0428—dc22   2008019164

This book is printed on acid-free paper.

08   09   10   11   12   10   9   8   7   6   5   4   3   2   1

Acquisitions Editor:	Dan Alpert
Editorial Assistants:	Tatiana Richards and Megan Bedell
Production Editor:	Veronica Stapleton
Copy Editor:	Amy Rosenstein
Typesetter:	C&M Digitals (P) Ltd.
Proofreader:	Dennis W. Webb
Indexer:	Sheila Bodell
Cover Designer:	Jeffrey Stith
Graphic Designer:	Scott Van Atta

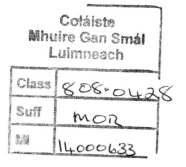

Contents

Acknowledgments

This book was inspired by many, many children and educators who have taught me what it means to be a teacher of writing. I would like to thank the school community at Corona Ave. Elementary for welcoming me into their school. Mr. Jack Baumann, thank you for always believing in my work and its impact on students. A special thank-you to Mr. Leo Machado, Mrs. Angelica Machado, and their students during the 2006–2007 school year. Their doors were always open, giving me complete access to the amazing work they were doing in writing. The students were always eager to share their writing with a sense of pride and accomplishment.

A special thank-you to Angelica Machado for all of her involvement in the development of this book. She is always willing to take risks in her teaching to ensure that all her students have an opportunity to learn. She has shared lessons, resources, and samples over the last ten years that have contributed to this book in many ways. And with all she has shared she further provided written and verbal feedback on draft after draft of this book. I am forever grateful to have her in my life as we continue to grow as educators together. Thanks also to Dan Alpert at Corwin Press for his availability and guidance throughout the publishing process.

To my past and present students, thank you for influencing my work as a teacher through your stories, your struggles, and your insights. So much of what I have come to understand about teaching writing came from the past ten years of working with children. From my youngest writers at PS 163 and Corona Ave. Elementary to my adolescent writers at IS44, I learned how to become a more effective teacher of writing. Thank you all for teaching me that my work as a teacher begins anew every year, with each class I teach and every new book I read.

To my family, the Mora bunch who were the inspiration for my own stories. And to my husband, Rudy, and daughter, Emilia, who add new inspiration every day. Marisol, thank you for keeping me company when I had to write, don't forget how loved you are and that writing can be your sanctuary.

Corwin Press wishes to acknowledge the following peer reviewers for their editorial insight and guidance.

James Becker, Teacher/Administrator
Toronto, Ontario, Canada

Ann C. Edmonds, Retired English
   Language Program Director/
   Teacher and Consultant
School District of Clayton, Clayton, MO

Rachel A. Mederios, ELL Teacher/
   Program Supervisor
Jefferson Elementary School,
   Boise, ID

Kelly Turcotte, Fourth Grade Teacher
Eccles Elementary School, Canby, OR

About the Author

Eugenia Mora-Flores is an assistant professor of clinical education in the Rossier School of Education at the University of Southern California (USC). She teaches courses on first and second language acquisition, and methods courses in literacy development for elementary and secondary students. Eugenia also serves as the coordinator of the bilingual and cross-cultural program, where she teaches a course on Latino culture in addition to supervising graduate students in the field. Her research interests include studies on effective practices in developing the language and literacy skills of English learners in grades K-12. Her recent publications include a coauthored book, *Balanced Literacy for English Learners* (K-2). Eugenia further works as a consultant for a variety of elementary and middle schools in the areas of English language development, specially designed academic instruction in English, and writing instruction for English learners (ELs). Eugenia is affiliated with the USC Center on Educational Governance (CEG), where she acts as principal translator for bilingual products developed for charter school communities, and serves as the chief liaison between CEG and the Spanish-speaking families with whom the center works. As a doctoral chair, Eugenia works with a group of students conducting research on teaching and learning with ELs. Research includes studies investigating writing instructional practices and programs for ELs, second language anxiety, two-way immersion programs at the middle school level, and elementary language arts programs for ELs.

Introduction

Writing became a passion of mine to teach when a teacher in high school told me that I wasn't a good writer. Initially, when I was in school I found writing to be pretty easy and I actually thought I was good at it: until my advanced placement (AP) American history teacher showed me otherwise. I failed my first history essay for the class. My teacher, Mrs. Witcop, explained that I had no thesis, my supporting paragraphs were disorganized, and I presented a weak conclusion. I was shocked! I had been writing formally in school for 10 years and no one ever told me I was doing anything wrong. I felt embarrassed. Here I was in an AP course and I didn't even know how to write a thesis statement. For the entire semester, Mrs. Witcop worked with me after class teaching me what a persuasive, literary essay was supposed to look like. We started with learning how to develop a thesis. Once she approved my thesis statement she guided me through the structure of the essay. I was so grateful for her help. I had learned the basic structure for academic writing. She taught me the foundation that guided my writing development through graduate school. The process Mrs. Witcop shared with me, analyzing the elements and structure of a type of writing, has inspired my work with writers to date.

For the past ten years, I have been learning how to teach writing. Specifically, I have worked alongside English learners (ELs) as we navigate through the complexities of written English. My instruction begins with understanding my students as second language writers. This was what Mrs. Witcop did for me. For teachers of ELs, this includes learning what your students are able to do as writers in both their first and second language. Knowing where you are starting from can lead to better instructional decisions.

My first year teaching I was fortunate to have worked directly with staff developers from the Lucy Calkins Reading and Writing Project in New York City. This experience opened my eyes to what children can do as writers. I began to read books on writing, one of my favorites being Katie Wood Ray's *Wondrous Words: Writers and Writing in the Elementary Classroom*. This book along with others helped me begin to understand what is involved in developing writers. I implemented a Writer's Workshop model in my classroom and engaged my students in author studies and multiple writing celebrations. At the time, I was teaching a first grade, dual-language class and my students learned to write in both English and Spanish. My students were amazing writers. My principal would often compliment our work posted in the hallways, and I was encouraged to submit my students' work for publication. I often regret that I never made copies of their writing to keep as a memoir of my first endeavors as a teacher of writing. A year later, I decided to take a risk and move on to middle school.

Knowing I would be working with adolescents I turned to another mentor author for help. Nancie Atwell's *In the Middle* and *Lessons That Change Writers* gave me so many ideas of how to approach writing with adolescents. And in teaching sixth, seventh, and eighth grades I began to understand that any great lesson I read about in books is contingent upon the students. I learned to make adjustments based on what my students were able to do in language and literacy. I learned a great deal about the struggles of teaching writing; struggles that at times were disheartening but necessary to truly understand what it meant to develop great, individual writers. These challenges made me better as a teacher, and my students became writers. For the first time, I felt successful as a writing teacher. I had developed a strong conceptual framework for teaching writing that I thought would work in any classroom. This was true until I hit a major roadblock when I moved back home to Los Angeles, California.

When I moved back to Los Angeles, I began teaching a bilingual first grade class. Fifteen of my students were to receive English instruction while the remaining five signed waivers to receive Spanish instruction. This was just after the passage of Proposition 227 in California, calling for structured English immersion (SEI) for all students. Structured English immersion requires all students to be instructed in English with modifications and instructional strategies implemented to meet the language needs of students, including but not limited to specially designed academic instruction in English (SDAIE) strategies. These strategies help make content comprehensible to students so that learning may occur. My class was the last of the first grade bilingual classes remaining at the school. More specific, the five "waiver" students were the last to receive bilingual education at the school to date. The challenges with teaching writing that I faced were not from my "waiver" students. Actually my five "waivers" achieved the highest levels in Spanish and English literacy on all schoolwide and statewide assessments that year. This was similar to my experience with my first graders in New York. Because they were taught in a dual-language model, they were able to develop their primary language literacy skills, which transferred effectively to their English language and literacy development.

My struggles were in teaching written English to the other fifteen ELs receiving all-English instruction. I used all of the writing methods and strategies I learned and practiced in New York, but they were not as effective. I began to think about how I could implement the same rich writing program in ways that would meet the language needs of my ELs. I had many conversations with a friend of mine who at the time worked as a staff developer for Lucy Calkins. We talked about her work with ELs in New York and mine with Spanish-speaking ELs in California. These conversations led to us writing a book, *Balanced Literacy for English Language Learners* (Chen & Mora-Flores, 2006), that addresses the language and literacy needs of ELs within a balanced literacy program. One chapter in the book, "Writer's Workshop," encapsulates the conversations we had around writing with ELs. The chapter provides an overview of Writer's Workshop and how to accommodate ELs during each component of workshop. This book, *Writing Instruction for English Learners,* goes further with writing. It attempts to address "what" students are writing and "how" to support ELs when writing various types of text in English. Its purpose is to *show* students how written English is organized for different purposes. It is the result of my struggles and successes working with ELs to develop their written English skills.

When I was learning to write with my history teacher, she showed me "what" a persuasive literary essay looked like. She highlighted the elements of a persuasive argument and broke down the parts of the essay. I had not taken time to really analyze and understand the type of writing I was asked to complete. To date, whenever I am asked to write a certain "type" of writing for a particular purpose, I begin by analyzing models. I look at how the text is typically organized and what kind of information is included. I make my doctoral students do the same when preparing to write their dissertations. They begin by reading dissertations and analyzing the different chapters. This helps guide their writing. The same is true for our youngest writers as well. All students need to be exposed to various types of writing and their genres. If students read wide and often, then this exposure comes easy. However, while students engage in these vicarious learning opportunities, when teaching ELs at different levels of second language acquisition, teachers must explicitly teach students to *see* writing.

To facilitate second language writing development for ELs I employ a constructivist approach to teaching writing. This includes providing the scaffolds and supports that ELs need to develop written English in a collaborative setting. Based on what my students are able to do as writers, I work toward taking them further in their writing development. Lev Vygotsky (1962) in his theories of learning explained that learning occurs best within a student's Zone of Proximal Development (ZPD). A student's ZPD is their learning curve; it accounts for what they are able to do independently and what they can do with the support of a more knowledgeable other. This support, also referred to as ***scaffolds***, involves the means by which a teacher provides the help (or mediates the help) students need based on their actual, current development. In the case of writing, scaffolds can include looking closely at the elements of written text, working alongside peers, and learning from models. Each type of text, narrative, expository, persuasive, and poetry, is analyzed for its elements and structure. An emphasis on the scaffolds students need to be successful within and across each type of text is presented throughout this book. It is through these scaffolds that my English learners have been successful in their development of written English.

Chapter 1, "Writing Instruction for English Learners," provides an overview of my understanding of how to teach writing to ELs. It includes a look at the development of second language writers in language-rich contexts. In addition, you will have a better understanding of how I approach written and literary genres. Each chapter thereafter will take you deeper into written text and genres.

Chapters 2 through 4 follow a similar format. Each chapter focuses on a type of writing, narrative, expository, and persuasive. You learn about the elements of selected written genres with each type of text. A detailed instructional sequence is then presented to show "how" to scaffold the writing for English learners. You will also find some fun ideas for publishing writing that I hope will motivate your students to want to write.

Chapter 5 on poetry has a bit of a different structure. Because there is no one general structure for writing poetry, I provide a variety of poetic forms. What makes poetry fun for ELs is the exploration of language. They get a chance to play with words and syntactic structures. In addition, the forms of poetry provide clear directions of how to craft a variety of poems.

What you will notice as you move from one chapter to the next is the focus on understanding the elements of written genres. I believe that as teachers, the more we know and understand about written English, the better we are at teaching writing. I strongly believe that the work of this book is just a starting point for developing writers. The discourse structure presented for each type of text is just a framework for ELs. As they continue to read in English and are exposed to a variety of written text, they will develop their own style and structure. I encourage students to experiment as writers with ideas, grammar, structure, and words. However, for ELs, they are just beginning to understand how written English works. For this reason, I carefully scaffold every step of the development of their written texts. But these scaffolds are presented with a great deal of choice and personal investment by the students. They will always use their own language to write their stories and will always be given a choice in what to write about.

Throughout the book I refer to student's English language development by the following second language acquisition (SLA) levels:

- *Level 1: Preproduction or Silent Stage:* at this stage ELs are active listeners, trying to understand their new language and surroundings. They will typically communicate through gestures, pointing, drawing, or nodding. As writers, ELs will often draw or sketch their stories.

- *Level 2: The Early Production Stage:* at this stage ELs are able to understand more oral and written English. "During this stage students are understanding more oral language and can usually speak and write in one or two word phrases and simple sentences related to social, everyday events" (Chen & Mora-Flores, 2006, p. 26). As writers, students will usually continue to draw but will begin to add text to support their illustrations by labeling, using simple words and phrases, and using phonetic spelling.

- *Level 3: The Speech Emergence Stage:* at this stage ELs can engage in dialogue and conversations. They can write multiple sentences and can understand abstract concepts. Since they are still developing their oral and written fluency, frequent corrections are not encouraged at this stage.

- *Level 4: The Intermediate Fluency Stage:* at this stage students can express their abstract thoughts and feelings in oral and written English. They can create multiple paragraph essays and have a command of English around social and familiar contexts.

- *Level 5: Native-Like Fluency:* at this stage ELs have a strong command of oral and written English. They are continuing to develop abstract, content-rich, academic language. "Students are able to produce oral and written language using a variety of grammatical structures and vocabulary comparable to their English-only peers" (Chen & Mora-Flores, 2006, p. 29). As writers, students are working toward developing a personal craft and style as writers across genres.

These levels are not meant to be static. Students can move across these levels at different rates and may exhibit different language capabilities within any one of the levels. In addition, they do not present the cognitive capabilities of the students. Meaning, all ELs possess a strong level of primary language acquisition, including both formal and informal language and knowledge. The SLA levels are intended to demonstrate what an EL is able to produce in a *second* language. In many cases, ELs will be able to think, write, and talk at levels much higher than what is explained, but in their first language. For example, students may be able to write craftily and creatively in their primary language but may still be at an "early production" level of SLA. This means they do not possess enough English language, yet, to express their thoughts orally or written *in English.* Through the book I will consistently present students' SLA levels to help you understand where the students are in their English writing development. This does not include what the students are able to produce in their primary language.

This book can be helpful when teaching writing to students in second through eighth grades. Though the work can be modified to work with younger students, I focus on second through eighth grades because students have developed strong literacy skills and can engage in the evaluative and analytic work of looking at written discourse. In addition, many of the lessons require a great deal of independence appropriate for these grade levels. Further, starting in second grade we see a greater emphasis in the standards on process writing, including revision and editing. It is here that we start to see students held accountable for writing across and within a variety of written genres.

This book is not intended to be a text on second language writing development, but a guide for teachers to understand written and literary genres. If teachers can look analytically at the way in which the English language is written for different purposes, we can do a better job of guiding ELs to write in English.

To my sister, Angelica, who gives every child a chance to succeed.

Writing Instruction for English Learners

1

Photo by Eugenia Mora-Flores.

All students possess the key ingredient for writing: ideas. Writing is grounded in the lived experiences of children. Our work as teachers of writing is to help students put these experiences down on paper in creative and articulate ways. "Currently, there is agreement (at least among researchers) that writing is a socially-constructed, meaning-making process. That is, writing is influenced and supported by writers' social and cultural experiences" (Davies-Samway, 2006, p. 17). We need to help students see the value of their lived experiences as the foundation for becoming great writers.

For English learners (ELs), the challenge lies in transferring their experiences into writing in a second language. As writers, ELs are rich with ideas and writing abilities from their first language. Through exposure to written text and formal instruction in their primary language, ELs are highly knowledgeable about how to write and write well. What makes it difficult for ELs is finding the medium and structure in English to express themselves effectively. As teachers we need to begin by understanding the process for developing writing in a second language as well as the instructional practices that best support that process.

PROCESS VERSUS PRODUCT

Our goal as teachers of writing is to develop the writer (Pressley, Mohan, Fingeret, Reffitt, & Raphael-Bogaert, 2007). We want students to understand what it means to be a writer—what it means to take an idea and, through careful planning and ongoing decision-making, turn it into a story, a poem, an essay, or a text. For the past thirty years, this idea of the importance of sharing with children the process of writing has helped teachers find more effective ways of developing writers. "Beginning in the 1970s, a focus on the cognitive processes involved in writing began to replace a focus on product and methodology" (Davies-Samway, 2006, p. 3). With this came the understanding that we need to teach children how to write, not just what to write.

Prior to the focus on process writing, writing instruction focused heavily on the perfection of a final piece of writing. Too often, teachers were the ones doing all of the hard work, while students sat back and just fixed the corrections suggested by the teacher. Writing instruction often followed a format similar to this: children were given a prompt, wrote a draft, teachers revised and edited the draft, students simply changed what the teacher said to change and resubmitted. If it wasn't good enough the teacher would edit again, and the student would copy the corrections until the final draft met the teacher's expectations. This practice failed to develop writers. When students received corrections from their teachers, they simply fixed the mistakes, often failing to notice the types of mistakes they were making. Teachers spent countless hours reading drafts and went through packs of red ink pens practicing their editing skills. In the end what mattered most was whether the child was able to recopy a perfect piece of writing.

I was guilty of this practice when I first started teaching middle school. I taught a sixth grade humanities class where history and language arts were integrated. As part of the course students wrote various texts, including historical fiction, poetry, and simulated autobiographies. After students submitted a first draft I would spend hours at home editing their papers. I wrote ideas in the margin of what they could add and corrected grammar and spelling. I would give my students their papers back, and in draft after draft they were only making the changes I fixed. From one writing sample to the next I saw the same mistakes being made over and over again. I realized that I was not teaching writing strategies and skills to develop writers. I was simply fixing the writing.

I needed to show students how to make decisions around content, style, and grammar for themselves.

With process writing, teachers SHOW children how to find mistakes, how to improve their writing, and how to make decisions about style and structure. English learners are given a chance to experiment with language and feel safe making mistakes along the way. Process writing helps us see how our ELs are developing their written English. We can see their learning through the errors they make. In the end the final draft shows us what the child is able to do as a writer. It may not be perfect, but it shows thought and their development of written English. In addition, ELs feel successful as writers because we celebrate the progress they have made as writers.

WRITING PROCESS

A popular teaching practice in schools to facilitate an understanding of how writing works is taking children through the five stages of the writing process: prewriting, drafting, revising, editing, and publishing. Often children are exposed to the five stages as a linear process whereby a writer goes from one step to the next without coming back to previous steps as a piece of writing is developed. Charts that display the writing process often create a visual of this linear concept for children because they will begin with prewriting and end with publishing (see Figure 1.1). When I read a book by Ralph Fletcher and JoAnn Portalupi titled *Writing Workshop: The Essential Guide*, they talked about writing being a cyclical process. As writers we very rarely proceed through a piece in such a finite, linear fashion. We jump around from drafting, to revising, then back to drafting, then edit a bit, going back to revision, stopping along the way to ask for help from friends or family. This iterative process and the role of others along the way is often absent in the linear process model. What I would propose, stemming from the work of Fletcher and Portalupi, is to present children the realities of writing as a cyclical process.

I created a classroom chart to produce a visual that represents this process (see Figure 1.2). Children need to understand that writing will take many decisions and many processes before arriving to a point where they are ready to share it with the world (publish). Many, many pieces will never even see the published stage because as writers we experiment with writing, we try out new things, and we practice. English learners will need lots of opportunities to do this, to practice their oral and written language as they work toward a piece they will want to share. In addition, they need ample opportunities to talk with classmates along the way at every stage of the process.

I don't want to mislead you into thinking that we should not teach children the five stages of the writing process; we will absolutely do so. But what I am suggesting is that they be taught as steps that will be taken over and over again, often with only one piece of writing. "Students grow as writers as they draft and redraft—as they tackle and solve revision problems" (Peitzman, 1992, p. 202). They will plan, draft, revise, and edit more than once on their way toward publication.

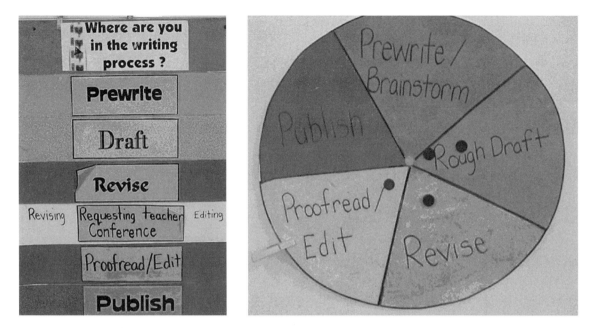

Figure 1.1 Linear Process Chart   **Figure 1.2** Cyclical Process Chart

Source: Figures 1.1 and 1.2 used with permission from Angelica Mora-Machado.

Figure 1.3, Stages of the Writing Process, explains my perspective on what can be taught at different stages of the writing process.

We take ELs through the process of writing with ongoing support from their teachers and peers. At every stage in the process students can respond to each others' ideas, style, and mechanics. This helps ELs feel supported as they try out written English in creative ways. If we wait until the end to engage in peer revision and editing, ELs might experience writing anxiety. They may feel isolated and alone in the process, causing apprehension for fear of writing incorrectly. Writing has been shown to cause second language learning anxiety (Kempf, 1995). Language development is negatively affected if students experience anxiety. Stephen Krashen (1981) explained in his *affective filter* hypotheses that in high anxiety, high stress learning environments ELs cannot effectively develop their second language. The language is not received by the learner, and so learning does not occur. For this reason it is critical to support ELs throughout the writing process by providing numerous opportunities to work alongside their peers. This support creates a sense of community and interdependence in a positive learning environment.

THE ROLE OF TALK

Though independent writing time is a private time to think and make personal decisions as writers, talk can foster language development and a supportive learning environment. "As they grow, writers still need opportunities to talk about what they are writing about, to rehearse the language of their upcoming

Prewriting	Generating ideas
	Selecting topics
	Quickwrite "mini-drafts" about personal experiences
	Draw or sketch an experience
	Setting a purpose for writing
	Identifying audience
	Identifying genre and its elements
	Organizing ideas (graphic organizers)
	Revising ideas on graphic organizers
	Exploring mentor texts to generate ideas for writing
	Exploring mentor texts to analyze discourse and text structure
	Notetaking
	Researching and collecting information
Drafting	Free-flow of ideas: trying out written language
	Identifying structure and purpose as you write: Scaffold the draft to understand the structure one paragraph at a time
	Peer discussion: reading for clarity along the way
	Peer discussion: crafting leads and conclusions along the way
	Applying elements of genre
Revising	Revisiting ideas for purpose, clarity, and effectiveness
	Adding information (details, examples, dialogue, facts)
	Adding descriptors (adjectives, adverbs, prepositional phrases)
	Adding sensory details
	Deleting repetition of ideas, words, phrases
	Substituting words (adjectives, repetitive function words, adverbs, pronouns, proper nouns, synonyms)
	Rearranging ideas with a focus on clarity and discourse (sequence, order of ideas, order of sentences, order of paragraphs)
	Adding an introduction, subheadings, closings/conclusion
	The language of genres: transition words, cue words, forms of language
Editing	Spelling
	Verb tenses
	Sentence structure
	Grammar, usage, and mechanics
Publishing	How will you share your writing with the world?
	Selecting a medium for publishing

Figure 1.3   Stages of the Writing Process

texts and run ideas by trusted colleagues before taking the risk of committing words to paper" (Writing Study Group of the National Council of Teachers of English [NCTE], 2004). English learners need to try out their English in a low-risk setting such as talking with a partner or small group. The exposure to academic talk, in this case around written English, facilitates language acquisition. Allowing opportunities for talk can happen at various times during writing instruction.

Before the students write independently they might discuss what they have been working on and gather suggestions from classmates on how to move forward with their writing. They can share ideas for future writing pieces or discuss their understanding of the mini-lesson of the day and how they might incorporate it into their own writing. *During* writing, students can talk with one another about choices they are making while they write. They might ask their neighbor their opinion about how something sounds, word choice, or ideas for character names or personalities. They can check their clarity by sharing what they have written and asking their neighbor to tell them what they understood and what suggestions they may have. *After* independent writing time children can talk about what they did that day as writers—what new strategies they tried out, what new words they learned and used, or simply share their writing. If students are asked to share their writing after independent writing time for peer feedback, I would suggest providing a short amount of time (two to three minutes) to note suggestions made by their partner. This notetaking can be done directly on their paper or on a sticky note to attend to the next day. This piece is important because ELs need time to process the feedback they received and make decisions about how to use it. If they don't have time to go back to their writing and make those decisions, they may forget what was suggested or forget to incorporate the feedback altogether. For this reason I strongly suggest that when giving children an opportunity to talk as writers, if the intention for talk is for feedback to improve a piece of writing, then it should be done *during* writing to provide opportunities for processing the feedback. Figure 1.4, The Role of Talk in Writing, gives an overview of the various ways in which teachers can engage students in talk during writing instruction.

As a teacher, you will decide at what point during writing you will allow children to talk. Though I always encourage them to help each other out during independent writing time, I remind students that their neighbors as well as themselves need time to write. We want to spend most of our time writing and, when necessary, we can interrupt our writing to ask our neighbors for help. If you feel that your students need more structure for "talk," I have also provided mini-lessons on how to engage in a dialogue around writing. I'll even direct students when they are allowed to talk. If they have questions prior to "talk time," they can tag them (with a small sticky note), and when it's time to talk, they can get right to their questions. Or, it may be that you mix it up. Some days you give students freedom to talk as needed, and other days you guide "talk time." It is a decision that will come from knowing your class. But, in any case, ELs need time to talk to facilitate language development as well as improve their writing skills.

It is often easier and more comfortable as a new speaker of a language to talk with a partner than to have to ask your questions out loud in front of the entire class. We want to give ELs the kind of learning environment and

When	Why (Purpose)	How
Before	Plan for writing	Share ideas for what to write about
		Share what they will work on as a writer that day
		Discuss the mini-lesson of the day and its application to their writing
During	Making decisions as writers	Stop and check for comprehension and clarity (Does this sound OK to you?)
		Discuss word choice, share vocabulary
		Elicit ideas for structure (Does this sound right here, or should I move it?)
		Help with spelling and mechanics
After	Sharing your work as a writer	Read your text to your partner
		Share any new strategies, words, ideas, or techniques you used this day
		Reflect on your day as a writer
		Provide feedback on the application of the day's mini-lesson to the writing
		Provide suggestions for improvement

Figure 1.4   The Role of Talk in Writing

opportunities where they can feel comfortable. They need to feel safe making mistakes and admitting that they "don't know" and need help. Stephen Krashen (1981) explains that in order for input (in this case language, both oral and written) to be understood and learned by an EL, it must be presented in a low-anxiety, comfortable environment for risk taking. He explains that a child's *affective filter* must remain low so that learning will occur.

DEVELOPING WRITTEN ENGLISH

Initially what ELs will rely on when writing is their development of basic inter-personal communication skills (BICS) (Cummins, 1984). This is the social language that children "pick up" as they talk with friends and are exposed to English. This language of social contexts is what transfers to students' writing. They utilize their BICS and their experiences to get them started writing in English. Then as they learn language in school through reading and across subject areas, they begin to develop their cognitive academic language profi-ciencies (CALP) (Cummins, 1984). Part of students' CALP is the language of written English. Students need explicit instruction on how written English is organized for a variety of purposes. This includes knowledge of the structure and elements of written and literary genres in English. In addition, the vocab-ulary, transition words, and language cues associated with different writing genres must further be taught and learned. And though CALP may take from seven to ten years to develop (Collier, 1987; Collier & Thomas, 1988), research shows that ELs can write very craftly and strategically prior to developing high levels of English language proficiency (Davies-Samway, 2006). We want to help ELs explore written English and provide opportunities for them to work through the stages of writing development in a second language. We need to provide the outlet for ELs to share ideas in a written form appropriate for their English language development level.

Stages of Written Output for English Learners

As ELs continue to develop their oral language skills, their writing will improve. Figure 1.5, Written Output Development for English Learners, is an example of how we can think about the development of second language writers. It shares examples of how ELs can express themselves in written form. However, it is necessary to note that these stages do not mean children are learning to write for the first time. They are examples of how ELs are transferring their experiences and knowledge about writing from a first language to a second language.

Written Output	Foundational Knowledge, Skills, Strategies, and Application
Drawing	Expressing ideas through images Using prior experiences and background knowledge from a primary language (L1) to express their ideas in written form, pictures, and images
Labeling/creative spelling	Applying content words (vocabulary) to drawings Applying their knowledge of L1 written forms to secondary language (L2) written forms to attempt to spell English words—transferring their knowledge of letters and sounds from one language to another As children read and are exposed to function words, they will apply them where applicable
Sentences	Apply their knowledge of simple English syntax to express complex ideas and experiences in simple sentences They can include multiple sentences, but they will be written in connected simple sentences
Multiple complex sentences	Apply their knowledge of English syntax to express and connect complex ideas and experiences in multiple sentences This will include an increase in the use of academic language, transition words, and the use of complex, compound sentences Apply their knowledge of paragraph structure
Stories/texts	Apply their knowledge of English syntax and discourse to organize longer stretches of text Use their knowledge and familiarity with stories and text from their primary language to guide them when writing in English Use their knowledge of genre, story grammar, and discourse

Figure 1.5 Written Output Development for English Learners

These stages are not based on any grade level. They represent how ELs can represent their ideas in English based on their second language development. These methods of written output are not representative of what students can do with writing in a primary language. Ideally, whenever possible we should always continue to develop students' primary language writing abilities because their cognitive proficiencies around writing will transfer to their work in written English. Jim Cummins (1984) refers to this as a students' common underlying proficiency (CUP). For example, if students learn about narratives and how to write a narrative in their primary language, they will not have to relearn the purpose and concept of narrative writing. They will, however, have to learn how it is typically structured in English and the words to use to represent their ideas in English. It is not about relearning a concept, but understanding how they are orchestrated in different languages.

Written Syntax and Discourse

All languages have common characteristics. They all possess a uniform, socially constructed manner in which the language is organized and expressed. These characteristics, often called components, include phonology, orthography, morphology, syntax, semantics, pragmatics, and discourse (see Figure 1.6, Components of a Language). Though ELs will need to be exposed to, learn, and practice all components of the English language, when writing it is often the syntax and discourse of the English language that they struggle with the most. Researcher and linguist Noam Chomsky (1972) believes that as humans, we are predisposed to language—that within our psyche we contain a language acquisition device (LAD), which codes for the proper structure of our developing language. More important, Chomsky believes that the development of language is a natural process that develops quickly in children through mere exposure. An infant is often exposed to very simple, often poorly structured pieces of language and yet is able to develop highly sophisticated language at an early age. For example, if a parent says to a child, "Bring me your shoes," the child, having been exposed to the English construction of this sentence, can naturally identify the English syntax (how the sentence is organized) to create new sentences using the same construct. He might say, "Mommy, bring me my book," or, "Daddy, bring mommy her purse." The child is using his knowledge of syntax with his knowledge of words to create many new and original sentences.

Chomsky believes that this process happens naturally as children are exposed to the language. And part of this process involves making mistakes. He explains that children will make mistakes as they overgeneralize rules (syntax). However, through further exposure and with the help of school, they will learn to develop highly complex, English syntax. When we hear a child say, "I goed to the bathroom," Chomsky would say it is a natural part of the acquisition process where we see evidence that a child has taken his knowledge about the use of past tense -ed endings to express a past event. English learners experience the same tendencies when learning English language syntax (rules of grammar) in school. They will overgeneralize the rule until they have been exposed to the exceptions, to new English syntax to regulate their incorrect tendencies. English learners will need exposure to the English language in a variety of contexts. They need to see the similarities and differences of English syntax within and across types of text. It is through this exposure that ELs will learn when and how to use words and generate sentences properly.

In addition, ELs need direct instruction on the written discourse structures of school. Throughout their educational careers, students are required to read and write a variety of written and literary genres. From narrative stories to persuasive essays, students need to learn the differences in the discourse structure from one type of text to another. "The degree to which discourse is planned reflects the extent to which the speaker or writer is able to consider, reflect on, organize, and revise the meanings to be conveyed. Forethought is the critical element" (Kucer, 2005, p. 49). Pauline Gibbons (1993), in her book *Learning to Learn in a Second Language,* further explains the importance of bridging the connection between oral and written English through a close look at the written discourse and syntactic structures of written genres. "The way that genres are organized is not the results of arbitrary rules, but a reflection of the way that a particular language is organized to fulfill specific purposes . . . each type of text or genre has its own particular language features which a writer must understand" (p. 105). For example, ELs will learn that when writing a narrative, they would typically begin by introducing the setting and characters, followed by the development of a plot, and ending with a resolution—all of which must be exposed to ELs through literature and taught directly through mini-lessons and modeled writing.

Keith Stanovich (1986) and Stephen Krashen (2004) have written at great lengths about the impact of reading on the development of language and literacy. When children read, often they are exposed to diverse ways in which language is organized and expressed. Through reading, children see how vocabulary is used, how authors chose to organize their ideas, and how the

Component	Concept/Definition
Phonology	The sound system of a language. How letters and sounds are articulated to form spoken language and generate meaning.
Orthography	The written system of a language. In English it is the alphabet.
Syntax	The structure of a language. How sentences are constructed to form coherent, logical sentences.
Semantics	The meaning system of a language. The denotations and connotations of words in social and cultural contexts.
Morphology	The smallest unit of meaning. How words are put together to form meaning. Includes roots, base words, prefixes, and suffixes.
Pragmatics	How language is understood and used in varying contexts.
Discourse	How longer stretches of written and oral language are organized. Includes the discourse of conversations as well as knowledge of genre.

Figure 1.6   Components of a Language

English language works when written, including syntax and discourse. Along with free-voluntary reading, teachers need to teach children how to read with attention to the discourse structure and craft of a piece of written text.

Lucy McCormick-Calkins (1994) talks about a writer's craft using a seamstress analogy. For example, when you or I go into a store to buy clothes, we may often simply look at how an item of clothing looks aesthetically—is it a good color for me, does it fit, is it my style? However, a seamstress may look at the same piece of clothing very differently. The seamstress may pay more attention to how it is put together, what stitching was used, do the colors selected and material go together, will it hold up wash after wash? This attention to the craft, how the article of clothing was put together, how ideas and decisions were made when creating the piece, is how one looks craftly at something. The same can be said about writing. When we read a book there are a variety of ways to read it. We might read for pleasure, for information, or to get ideas for writing. When writers read, they pay attention to how the text is written. They see new ways of thinking about writing, new ways of crafting their ideas to express themselves with more clarity and purpose.

Teachers need to demonstrate for children how to read like a writer. Through modeled writing and read-alouds, teachers can show children *how* authors write. In addition, ELs need to see how texts are organized in English for a variety of purposes. For example, they need to know how narrative writing is organized and how it is structured to convey meaning. The same is true for all genres of writing in English. Because the development of a writer involves knowledge of syntax and discourse to express ideas clearly in writing it will be the responsibility of the teacher to show them how to read with an eye toward syntax and discourse.

Understanding Genre

Throughout the book I will follow an understanding of genre based on the book *Dimensions of Literacy* by Stephen Kucer. Kucer explains that written text can be classified by type, genre, and structure. Types are the broader categories of written text, including narrative, expository, persuasive, and poetic. Within each text type there are genres that fit within the context and construct of each type. A genre is a kind of literary work using a particular form or technique. Meaning, each genre has a familiar organizational structure and common elements that help define the genre. Figure 1.7 is representative of some types of literary and written genres children are expected to read and write from second through eighth grade.

Figure 1.7 is not meant to be an exhaustive list. It presents a variety of written and literary genres that children write within and across. Some of those presented in the table will be further explained and developed in the chapters that follow. Each text type and genre will be presented with attention to its general characteristics and more specifically how it is organized (structure and discourse). Gibbons (1991) defines these general characteristics as language features that include "the overall structure or organization, the order of parts, and the specific grammatical features" (p. 105).

Type	Definition	Literary Genres
Narrative	Stories: can be fiction or nonfiction	Personal narratives Autobiographies Fairy tales Fables Folktales Fantasy stories Mysteries Myths Diaries
Expository	Provides Information	How-to texts Biographies Reports Articles
Persuasive	To inform, explain, convince, present a position, evaluate, or persuade	Letters Editorials Advertisements Essays/compositions Literary essay
Poetry	To express ideas both fictional and nonfictional in creative, often nonstandard ways	Free verse Pattern poems Haiku Acrostic poems Cinquain Diamante Limericks

Figure 1.7 Literary and Written Genres

CONCLUSION

Writing is a process by which we transfer our thinking, our ideas, and our experiences into written form. For ELs, their experiences and knowledge of the English language will serve as building blocks for writing. Teachers will in turn supply the context, the support, and the knowledge about how written English is structured and organized. As part of their knowledge of written English, teachers can further facilitate the development of academic language through explicit instruction on different types of written forms (e.g., narrative, expository, persuasive, and poetic) and their subsequent genres, all of which can be learned in a language-rich environment where students are given varied opportunities to talk about writing. Establishing a community of writers where students feel safe trying out language and making errors along the way is necessary for second language development. With careful attention to the role of structure and talk when writing, coupled with a cyclical approach to teaching writing, teachers will be better equipped to address the needs of their ELs.

Narrative Writing 2

Photo by Eugenia Mora-Flores.

*T*here was never a dull moment growing up with five siblings. We were always finding new and exciting ways of entertaining ourselves. From our own private indoor soccer arenas in the living room to lip singing competitions and your typical games of hide-and-seek, my memory is full of days of fun and laughter with my three brothers, Ismael, Ivan, and Isaac, and my two sisters, Adriana and Angelica. It was always the perfect number, six! We could play three against three or have enough for a group game with one person being "it" and five people to go after. And with only nine years between the oldest and the youngest, the competition always seemed fair.

Of all the games we made up and used to play, one of my favorite games as a child was "toro." I am sure you're thinking, "toro," hmm . . . a bull? What did we possibly do? Well here is how the game was played. Someone was the "toro" while the rest of us had to avoid being tagged by the "toro." Now the only way to get tagged *was if your feet were touching the ground. You see we played it in the living room where we used the couches, piano bench, and end tables as our sanctuary. So you had to leap or run as fast as you could from one couch to another and avoid being tagged by the "toro." We would chant "toro," "toro," to whoever was it, and because we were so young at the time, between four and thirteen years old, the distance from one couch to other seemed miles away. I can remember not wanting to be tagged while at the same time I liked being the "toro." We would play for what seemed like hours, going from one "toro" to another and all the while jumping up and down on the couches laughing and having a great time. I can't remember what brought the game to an end, except for maybe it was my mom telling us not to jump on the couches. But no matter how it came to an end there was always a sense of satisfaction when it was over and the end of one game was really only the beginning of another. We would put our heads together and think of a new way to keep ourselves busy without getting into trouble.*

When I think back to those days and share them with my husband, he often thinks we were a bunch of crazy kids, but I see it is a blessed childhood. To this day my siblings and I are still playing together, different kinds of games though, and are as close as ever. Part of my desire to share these stories is to share the beauty of having a large family and siblings to play with all the time. I share them because I hope that one day my daughter will have a chance to play these and the many games she will invent in the future!

—Mora-Flores, 2008

UNDERSTANDING NARRATIVE WRITING

We all have stories to share, and because of this we can all write narratives! When I was trying to think about which story from my life to share I realized how many stories we all truly have. Whether they are happy stories or sad stories, good stories or great stories, we all have stories because we all have lived.

Narrative writing tells a story by sharing the details of an experience. Narratives are the stories children love to hear, read, and enjoy. Though many narratives are accounts or recounts of things we have done or stories we have heard, our experiences also give us ideas for original stories. The following list details the main aspects of narrative writing:

- Can be fiction or nonfiction, based on personal experiences, inspired by personal experiences, or completely made up;
- Includes literary elements of plot, setting, and characters that are well defined and developed;
- Answers who, what, when, where, how, and why about something we have experienced or have created;
- Uses colorful details to help the reader share in the experience with you;
- Presents information logically (from beginning to end) while at the same time can be craftly written with flashbacks or cyclical plotlines;
- Contains dialogue (when appropriate) to provide insight into the thoughts and actions of the characters;

- Provides a point or theme to the story; and
- Can be written from any point of view.

A misconception about English learners (ELs) is that they cannot write until they have mastered at least a conversational level of the English language. However, as we noted in the opening chapter, all students have ideas for stories through their lived experiences. These experiences are not language specific; all students have gathered a vast amount of ideas from their lives to write about. What we need to do as teachers is to help them find the medium by which to share their stories in English. This includes allowing ELs opportunities to express themselves in creative ways (see Figure 1.5, Written Output Development for English Learners). They can begin by drawing or sketching their ideas. Eventually they will gradually transfer what they are learning in English, orally and in writing, to write words and stories. English learners need to feel safe playing with language to share their ideas in English. All the while teachers need to provide the models and exposure to written English to support this transfer and ongoing development.

Along with providing opportunities for risk taking and exploring language, teachers also need to equip themselves with the knowledge of how narrative writing works in English. As ELs develop their conversational English language skills, it is the responsibility of the teacher to help them develop their academic English, including how written English is created and organized. We need to become more knowledgeable about how to write narratives as well as understand the different subgenres within narrative writing and how they are typically written. Once we learn to *see* narrative text, we can in turn teach ELs the elements and generalizations of how to write each subgenre. The purposeful attention to the typical discourse structure of narrative genres is just a beginning; as students continue to read and *see* the English language, they will eventually develop their own style as writers.

NARRATIVE ESSAYS

Narrative writing can take on a variety of forms, but for the most part it involves the development of a story with particular elements. These elements are identified and described in Figure 2.1.

Literary elements that are used in the development of a narrative often occur in a certain part of the story. In the *beginning* of a narrative it is common to identify and describe the setting, introduce the characters, engage the reader with an enticing opening, and identify events leading toward a problem. In the *middle*, the problem is revealed and becomes worse, or additional roadblocks are set up to throw off the main characters' attempts to solve the problem. These roadblocks are helpful in writing more elaborative, interesting narratives. In the *end* the problem is resolved, and there is a resolution or point made about the story as a whole. This structure is also referred to as "story schema." Figure 2.2 summarizes the "story schema" of a narrative.

English learners need to be exposed to the story schema of narratives to continue their academic language development. Teachers can present this

16

Literary Element	Description	Evidence
Setting	Provides the backdrop for your story Limited sketching of when and where the story is taking place: 1. Location 2. Weather 3. Time period (when I was 5, during the Civil War, back in 1999. . .) 4. Time of day (in the morning, one evening) 5. Passage of time (a week later, after a while, now)	Can be realized through characters' clothes, technology, dates, tools, daily living, laws, housing, historical references, description of landscape, transportation
Character	People or personified animals. Developed through: 1. Appearance 2. Action (helps you learn about them) 3. Dialogue 4. Monologue (thoughts)	By what the author or narrator tells you By what the character does, says, or thinks By what other characters say, do, or think about the character
Plot	The development of a story from beginning to end The pattern of events introduction, problem, climax, resolution	Plot can develop: 1. Between character(s) and nature 2. Between a character and society 3. Between characters
Point of View	The perspective from which the story is being told	Within a character 1. First person: Narrator is usually the main character, told through the eyes of one character (pronoun: *I*) 2. Omniscient: Godlike, seeing and knowing all, the author tells readers about the thoughts of the character(s) (pronoun: *you*) 3. Third person/limited omniscient: Readers know the thoughts of the character(s) (pronouns: *he, she, they*) 4. Objective: Readers are eyewitnesses to the story. Focus is on recounting events (e.g., fairy tales)
Theme	Underlying meaning of the story, can embody general truths about human nature Common to have several themes in one story	Implicit (inferred) Explicit (stated openly, e.g., fable)

Figure 2.1   Literary Elements

Beginning		Middle	End	
Background information	Rising action	Climax	Falling action	Resolution
Narration setting Foreshadowing characters	Events building up to a climax	Culminating event: The problem is realized in actions Conflict, tension or opposition	Events after the climax	The final action that resolves the conflict Theme, symbols, and/or truth revealed

Figure 2.2   Story Schema (Discourse)

schema through read-alouds. Students will be able to *hear* what a narrative story sounds like. In addition, shared reading, modeled writing, and shared writing can *show* students what narrative writing looks like. In all cases the teacher is providing heavy support to students as writers as the model of what narrative writing looks and sounds like. But in addition to the role of the teacher, it will ultimately be through reading wide and often that students will start to see alternative, creative ways of organizing a narrative, and they will soon begin to model their writing after favorite authors or stories (see Figure 2.3, Ways of Developing Plot). What teachers are doing initially is laying the foundation of the structure of a narrative essay (discourse).

Circular plotline	The main plot curves back to connect to the beginning. For example, the main character ends up back (the setting and time) to where the story began. Flashbacks are common in circular plots.
Cumulative plotline	Events accumulate ultimately leading to the climax and ending of the story. The main part or idea of the story is stationary with new actions added along the way.
Episodic plotline	Chronological story with separate episodes. Each episode has a conflict and resolution.
Linear plotline	A story unfolds according to a time sequence. For example it begins with Monday morning and ends on Friday night.

Figure 2.3   Ways of Developing Plot

To help you understand better how we as teachers can do a better job of guiding ELs through the process of writing a narrative, I provide an example of a comprehensive instructional writing sequence for personal narratives. This particular sequence has been used on many occasions with grades ranging from second through eighth. What will change from one grade level to the next is the stories selected to share as examples of narratives as well as the complexity of the grammar usage and mechanics lessons. Particular syntax and revision lessons are always dependent upon your students and their needs. This particular sequence was used with a third grade class of Spanish-speaking ELs at various stages of second language acquisition. What I hope you will focus on as you read through the lessons is how the structure (discourse) of the entire narrative is broken down for ELs to serve as a scaffold for developing a narrative. The structure of each lesson in the writing sequence, including introduction, mini-lesson, independent practice, and share, was derived from the work of Lucy McCormick-Calkins's (1994) writer's workshop. I have also noted the key objective for each lesson in the "mini-lesson."

(Text continued on page 27)

What Is a Narrative?

Introduction: Conduct an oral brainstorm with the class to answer the question, "What is a narrative?" Record the students' answers on a large chart paper.

Mini-lesson: **Collecting narratives from our lives**. Read *How I Spent My Summer Vacation* by Mark Teague. Model a web with the book that shows the who, when, where, what, how, and why of the book.

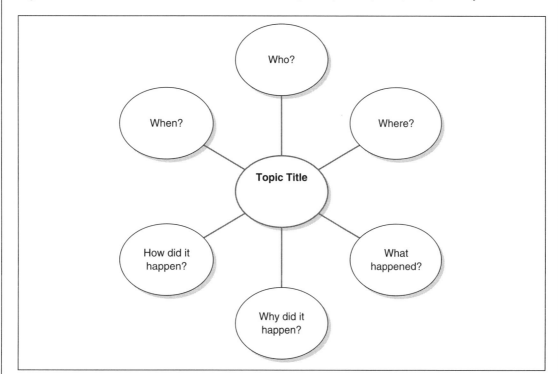

Explain to students that this book shared a story about something very familiar, summertime. "Today you are going to think about the stories from your life that you might want to share with us." Ask students to close their eyes and think as you take them through a series of brainstorming ideas and questions:

- Think about some special times you have spent with your family. Where did you go? What did you do?
- Think about some special days you have shared with your friends. What did you do?
- Think about the different holiday celebrations you have shared with your family. When was it? What did you do?
- What about some fun or even sneaky things you did with your brothers or sisters? What did you do?

Tell students to hold on to all of their ideas because they will be writing a list of their different ideas and experiences.

Independent writing: Students will list a series of possible topics or personal experiences they would like to write about. If they have difficulty writing, they can draw their experience or write their topic ideas in their primary language.

Share: Students will share their list with a partner. After sharing their list give them two to three minutes to add additional ideas.

Exploring Narratives

Introduction: "Yesterday we started thinking about the different stories from our lives. Today we are going to keep thinking about what we mean by a narrative." The teacher (orally or through an illustration) shares a personal story, making sure to address the who, when, where, what, how, and why of her story.

Figure 2.4 Instructional Writing Sequence for Writing Personal Narratives   *(Continued)*

(Continued)

Mini-lesson: **Understanding plot.** Read a short story from Gary Soto's *Baseball in April and Other Stories.* This book contains personal narratives from Soto's life as a child and an adolescent. His experiences are very familiar to kids, and his style of writing is very engaging and descriptive. After reading the story as a class complete a sequence chart for the plot of the story.

Beginning	Middle	End

Independent writing: Using their list of ideas from the day before, students will quickwrite one personal experience. If students finish earlier than the allotted time, have them write another quickwrite for another experience on their list.

Share: Students will read their quickwrite to a partner. The partner will identify the who, when, where, what, why, and how of the story he hears. Students will get about two to three minutes to go back to their quickwrite and add anything they thought was missing based on their partner's responses.

Introduction: "We will continue to explore different narratives and how they are written in a common sequence."

Mini-lesson: **Understanding plot.** Read another short story from Gary Soto's *Baseball in April and Other Stories.* After reading the story as a class, add a new row to the chart from the previous day, again sequencing the events of the story.

Beginning	Middle	End
1.		
2.		

Independent writing: Students use their list of ideas from the first day and quickwrite another personal experience. Again, if students finish early, then they select another topic and do an additional quickwrite. These quickwrites are simply a free flow of ideas as students try and remember the event or experience.

Share: The teacher will call on two to three students to read one of their quickwrites out loud. The class can share their thoughts and curiosities with the student. This is not a time for feedback from the class since students are simply brainstorming at this point. However, the teacher can point out the plot of the student's story to connect back to the mini-lesson.

Introduction: "Today we will look at one more story and continue to explore how it is written in a common sequence."

Mini-lesson: **Understanding plot.** Read another short story from Gary Soto's *Baseball in April and Other Stories.* After reading the story as a class, add to the chart from the previous day, again sequencing the events of the story.

Beginning	Middle	End
1.		
2.		
3.		

Independent writing: Once again students use their list of ideas from the first day and quickwrite another personal experience. Again, if students finish early, then they select another topic and do an additional quickwrite. By this time, all students will have at least 3 quickwrites of personal narratives they can select from to engage in the writing process.

Share: The students will share their quickwrite with a partner. Partners will retell the story they hear, focusing on the events that took place at the beginning, middle, and end.

Understanding Narratives

Introduction: Review the sequence chart from the past three days. "We have been looking at how Gary Soto develops his stories from beginning to end. Today we are going to look closer at the information he shares at the beginning of his stories."

Mini-lesson: **Understanding elements of plot.** Begin by asking the students to look at the column from the sequence chart that says Beginning. "What do you notice about the beginning of narratives?" Give students a chance to talk with a partner as they analyze the beginnings of Gary Soto's stories. Typically, by looking at the chart the class will notice that most of Soto's beginnings included character introductions, a description of the setting, and an introduction to the idea or topic of the story that he develops later. Record their responses on a large chart paper. Continue by asking students what they notice about what happens in the middle and end. Again record their responses onto the chart paper. Students will use this information as they begin to plan their personal narratives.

Modeled writing: The teacher will then model how to plan a narrative with attention to the elements of narrative and story schema. Using Resource A: Writing Personal Narratives, the teacher will plan out a personal narrative.

Independent writing: Students will take one of their quickwrites and plan out their narrative using Resource A: Writing Personal Narratives. If students finish early, then they can prepare another plan from another quickwrite. This allows all students time to complete at least one plan for a personal narrative. You want to emphasize to students that their work as writers is never finished. They will always work purposefully on new stories or improve current ones.

Share: Students will share with a partner what they have accomplished as a writer that day.

Developing Narratives: The Beginning

Introduction: "Now that we have planned out what we want to talk about in our personal narratives, today we will start drafting."

Mini-lesson: **Drafting the beginning.** Using her "Personal Narrative" graphic organizer, the teacher will model how to write the beginning of her own personal narrative. Remind students of the discussion on beginnings from the day before. In the beginning we typically describe the setting and introduce the characters and the event. Tell students that with their discussion of "beginnings" in mind, let their ideas flow. Drafting is how we take our ideas and organize them into a logical story without worrying too much at this point about perfection.

Independent writing: Students will use their graphic organizers and draft their beginnings. Again, if students finish early, then they can plan and prepare another story from their collection of quickwrites.

Share: Students will share with a partner their beginning. Their partner will identify the elements of narrative beginnings described in their partner's story. Allow students two to three minutes to add to their beginning based on their partner's feedback.

(Continued)

(Continued)

"The Opener"

Introduction: The teacher will read the beginning of her story and ask students their opinion on the effectiveness of her opening to capture their attention. Students should be asked to explain their thinking. "Did you like my opening? Why or why not? What could I do to make it better?" "Today we will leave our stories and look closer at some examples of how authors start their narratives."

Mini-lesson: **Introducing your story.** How can you capture your audience? The teacher will go back and re-read, out loud, the opening of the three Gary Soto stories read. She will share the kinds of openings they were and why they were effective.

Independent practice: With a partner students will be given a personal narrative to read. After reading the story they will write on a sticky note the opening of the story they read. Each partnership will decide what kind of opening it was and whether they thought it was a good opening. Ask partnerships to justify their opinions.

Share: Start by asking one partnership to read out loud their opening. Ask the class, "What kind of opening was it?" The teacher will write the type of opening and ask the partnership to place their sticky note under the heading as an example. Continue this process until all partnerships have shared. If a partnership has the same type of opening, then they will simply place their sticky note in the corresponding column. Your chart of possible opening types might be organized like the example below:

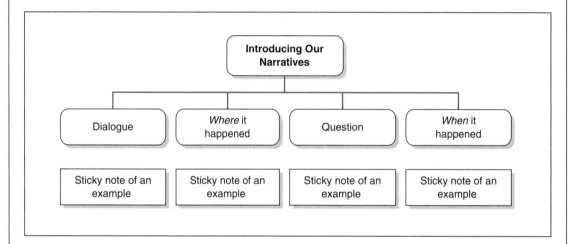

Students will not work on their own openings during this lesson. Close by revisiting and reminding the students about the many ways to introduce/begin/open a narrative.

Revising "Our Introductions/Openers"

Introduction: "So yesterday we took some time away from our drafts to look at the different ways authors open their stories. Today we are going to look back at our drafts of the beginning of our personal narrative and see if we can make them better."

Mini-lesson: **Revising introductions.** Using her personal narrative, the teacher will revisit her opening. The teacher will select two types of openings from the chart created the day before and create possible openings for her narrative. Model the thought process on how to select the right opening. One opening at a time, the teacher will reread the entire beginning of her draft to hear how each opening sounds. Ask the class which one they think sounds the best. The teacher will revise her opening based on the classes' feedback.

Independent writing: Students will create two different types of openings for their own personal narratives. They should read each opening with the rest of their beginning paragraph(s) to hear how each sounds.

Share: Students will share the opening they decided on with their partner and ask the following:

- What did my opening make you think about?
- Does it make you want to keep reading? Why?
- Do you have any ideas on how I can make it better?

Allow students two to three minutes to incorporate their neighbor's feedback.

Syntax

Based on your observation of your students' writing, what is the need at this point with syntax? This lesson will vary based on your students' needs. The reason for engaging in some syntax lessons at this point is to provide students with the skills they need as they continue to draft their stories. They will begin to apply their learning as they move their draft forward. They don't have to wait until the end. For example, you can do sentence lifting and engage students in syntactic analysis for developing correct "I" sentences.

Mini-lesson: **Sentence structure.** Personal narratives include many "I" sentences. The teacher will revisit her personal narrative and identify some of her "I" sentences. For example, the teacher can write the sentence, "When I was younger I loved playing outside." She would then ask the class to look closely at the sentence. "Who is this sentence about? What is the action or verb in the sentence? What is the person doing or talking about?" The teacher will summarize what the students noticed. "So in this sentence, I begin by using the word 'I' to tell you that this is a personal story, then I tell you what I liked doing, 'playing,' followed by where I liked to play, 'outside.' When you develop a sentence, you want to be sure you have the subject, who it is about, the verb, what they are doing, and add some details to make it a rich sentence, like where they are doing it, with who, or how they are doing it. Let me take another look at my sentence and see if I can make it even richer." The teacher will rewrite the sentence: "When I was younger I loved playing outside with my brothers and sisters." The teacher can go on to analyze and revise additional "I" sentences. Or you can ask students to share out some "I" sentences about personal experiences. Record the sentences on chart paper and have the class revise the sentences to make them correct, rich "I" sentences.

Independent writing: Direct the students to continue to develop their beginnings and think about how they can improve their "I" sentences. Ask them to select at least three "I" sentences to fix up or add to their narratives.

Share: Ask two to three students to share out loud great "I" sentences. Ask the class to comment on why they thought they were good, correct sentences.

Moving Our Draft Forward

Introduction: "We've spent some time improving the beginning of our personal narratives; I think we are ready to move forward with our stories."

Mini-lesson: **Drafting the middle.** "What do you notice about the middle of narratives?" By looking back at the chart the class filled out about Gary Soto's stories, students will notice that in the middle of the narrative the author reveals a problem and some obstacles for the main character(s). The teacher will revisit her graphic organizer (Resource A: Writing Personal Narratives) and identify the problem and at least three obstacles or events leading up to the problem. She will then model the middle of her draft. Ask students to think about how they will lead up to the problem and which roadblocks, challenges, or obstacles they will make their characters face.

Share: Students will share their graphic organizer with their partner; the focus will be on the middle of the plot. Partnerships will help one another identify at least three events leading up to the problem (climax).

Independent writing: Students will continue their drafts using their revised graphic organizer to flesh out the middle of their narratives.

Nearing the End

Introduction: "Now that we have led up to the problem, we need to start thinking about how we want to bring our stories to an end."

(Continued)

(Continued)

Mini-lesson: **Drafting the end.** "What do you notice about the end of narratives?" By looking back at the chart the class filled out about Gary Soto's stories students will notice that by the end of the narrative, the problem is solved and concluding thoughts are made.

The teacher will continue her narrative through modeled writing. Ask students to think about how they will solve the problem. Ask them to lead their audience toward the solution by presenting at least three events after the problem or conflict is identified. This helps students stretch out their stories. You can also ask them to wind down the story by adding three additional events or actions that happened after the solution.

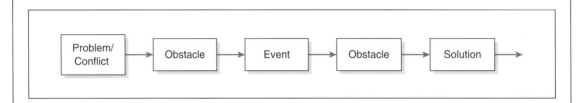

Independent writing: Students will first plan out their ending using a flow chart similar to the one above. Once they have decided how to stretch out the plot and bring their story to an end, they can continue their draft.

Share: Students will read their ending to their partner for feedback. Some questions they might ask their partner include:

- Is there something missing?
- Was there something you wanted to hear that you didn't?
- Do you have any ideas of what I can add to make it better?

Allow students two to three minutes to process and note the feedback they received.

Bringing Our Stories to an End

Introduction: Chart the classes' response to the question, "What happens after the problem is solved in a story?"

Mini-lesson: **Drafting the end.** Remind students that stories need to be concluded and not stopped. Many kids solve the problem and turn right to the end. Ask them to think about what they want their audience to think about at the end of the story. They can:

- Make a statement about the theme.
- End with a question to make the reader keep thinking.
- Write additional events that happened after the solution.
- Rewrite what the story was mainly about. For example, "And that was the day I first learned to ride a bike."
- Make a statement about a lesson learned.
- Explain why the story was so important to you as the writer.

The teacher will model her ending.

Independent writing: Students will continue to draft, revising their ending.

Share: Ask students to share their conclusion with a partner for feedback. Questions they might ask can include:

- What did it make you think about when I read the last line?
- Did you think it ended well or should I add more information before the last line?
- Any suggestions on how I can make it better?

Allow students two to three minutes to process and note feedback they received from their partners.

Revising the Draft: Descriptive Writing

Depending on what you have observed from your students writing you can decide what to focus on during revision. In all cases the teacher will use modeled writing to show students how to make their writing more descriptive.

Mini-lessons can include:

- **Sensory details.** Taking a sentence and expanding it using sensory details. For example: "It was a nice day," can be revised to read, "I could smell the fresh air, and feel the warmth of the sun on my skin as we walked toward mom's house." Questions students can ask themselves as they revise some of their sentences may include: What did you hear? What did you feel? Could you smell anything special that made you think or feel a certain way? What did you see around you?
- **Show not tell.** The when, where, why, and how of your ideas. Add more information that relate to the main idea. What else happened? Who else was there? What were they doing? How were you feeling? What were you thinking? What were the other characters doing? What happened on the way?
- **Add adjectives** to make the writing more descriptive. Be sure to use a rule of two. For example, "The fish are swimming," can become, "The <u>colorful</u>, <u>rainbow</u> fish are swimming quickly." This will keep their ideas from sounding extraordinary. Sometimes kids can get overzealous and write, "The big, cute, red, blue, yellow, smelly, slimy, stinky fish are swimming." To help students understand how to add adjectives properly to their writing, ask them to find and circle some main nouns and then have them add an adjective before the noun. This will remind them that one way we use adjective in English is by preceding the noun.
- **Add adverbs** to make the writing more descriptive. Be sure to be explicit as to how adverbs work. Explain to them that adverbs answer "how" something is done and that they can either precede or follow a verb. For example, "The fish <u>quickly</u> swam away from the shark," or, "The fish swam <u>quickly</u> away from the shark."
- **Add prepositional phrases** to expand ideas. For example: "The fish were swimming," can become, "<u>Throughout the day</u> the brave fish were swimming <u>in the ocean, next to a hungry shark.</u>" To add a preposition students can ask themselves where and when the event took place.
- **Replace overused words** (e.g., and, but, nice) with vivid words. Model alternatives to these words. The same can be done with overused, dull verbs. Provide students with a word bank of rich words and vivid verbs. The use of mentor authors for word choice is very helpful. Two of my favorite texts for teaching about overused words are *The Boy Who Cried Fabulous* by Lesléa Newman and *Crickwing* by Janell Cannon. In *The Boy Who Cried Fabulous,* Newman shows students how silly the repetitive use of a word can sound in a story and how they can find alternative words to use. *Crickwing* uses a variety of descriptors to introduce dialogue as opposed to using "said."
- **Add dialogue.** Review with students the grammar of dialogue, how to use quotation marks, punctuating dialogue, and the use of capital letters.
- **Adding transitions.** The chart below is helpful for guiding students to improve their transitions when writing narratives. A copy of the chart to distribute to your students is available in Resource B: Transitions for Narrative Writing.

Beginning	Middle	End
At first	After a short time	Happily ever after
At the beginning	Instantly	Last of all
Once upon a time	Just when	Finally
When I was . . .	Not long after	In the end
Back when I was . . .	Previously	At last
Far away	Recently	From that day on
Long ago	All at once	Since then
There is a place	In no time	After that I never (don't)
called . . . where . . .	Suddenly	In the future
	Afterwards	
	Following that	

These mini-lessons can be introduced to students as early as the drafting stage of the writing sequence. They can then be revisited when the draft is complete. You don't want to conduct them too early because the students need plenty of text to revise, but you may want to give them a chance to engage in revision

(Continued)

103514568

(Continued)

early enough so that they can apply what they are learning as they develop their stories. This decision will again be based on what you notice your students doing as writers.

Peer Revision

You need to be sure to model what good comments sound like during a peer session. Students can work with a partner on their final revisions, or you can separate the class into groups based on their revision needs. You might also choose to provide a guide for peer revision. You can create them to focus on specific mini-lessons you have covered. A sample peer revision guide is available in Resource C: Peer Revision Sheets. For some additional ideas for revising with students I encourage you to read *The Revision Toolbox: Teaching Techniques That Work* by Georgia Heard.

Editing

As students continue to work on revising their drafts, take note of the kinds of grammar, usage, mechanics, and spelling errors they are making. This will determine your editing mini-lessons. Some editing lessons I have used with my ELs have included:

Sight words. Locating function words or sight words the class has been working on and holding students accountable for the proper spelling.

Morphemic or spelling patterns. Have students find words that contain a common spelling or morphemic pattern the class has been working on. You will decide on which to focus based on what you have been working on during phonics or word work and the errors you've seen your students making in their writing. For example, if you notice many of your students misspelling words containing the morpheme -tion, you can engage the class in a lesson on when to use the spelling -sion and -tion. Ask students to look in their writing for words that contain the sound of the morpheme -tion and double-check that they have used the proper spelling.

Subject-Verb Agreement. Through sentence lifting, model improper and proper subject-verb agreement in a sentence. Use sentences from the students to review proper subject-verb agreement. Students will then be required to double-check their sentences for proper subject-verb agreement.

Punctuating Dialogue. Dialogue is a great way to improve narrative writing. For this reason a lesson that reviews how to punctuate dialogue properly is necessary.

Peer Editing

In triads you can engage students in a peer-editing session. I recommend triads to provide two pairs of eyes for this technical part of the writing. Each triad will be responsible for reading each others' paper and marking errors. You will want to review editing marks with the class as part of your mini-lesson. You can also focus the peer-editing session by asking students to focus on specific skills. Sample Peer Editing Sheets are provided in Resource D. I would also recommend *A Fresh Approach to Teaching Punctuation* by Janet Angelillo for additional ideas on editing.

Expanding Our Narratives

Give students time to work toward publication. They will continue to incorporate all of the previous mini-lessons, talk with their friends to improve their writing, and make final decisions before making their writing public. This can also include adding illustrations, or, if more drawing took place than writing during the lessons, students might want to try and add some text.

Independent Writing (The Work of a Writer Is Never Done)

When you think you are finished, go back to your quickwrites and begin to draft a new narrative from another one of your ideas. This gives other students time to finish publishing while making sure that everyone is working purposefully to develop themselves as writers.

Publishing

You will want to decide how students will make their writing public. Students can type out their narratives and add an illustrated title page or make a book out of their narrative. Whichever form of publication you chose, I find that students enjoy sharing their stories with others. An Author Celebration, where selected classes, administration, and families are invited to hear and read the students' stories, is a great way to wrap up a writing genre.

Many parts of the instructional writing sequence presented were developed with particular attention to the needs of ELs. Specifically, some elements of the instructional sequence that provided language and literacy scaffolds for ELs included:

- Multiple opportunities for students to explore narratives before writing one on their own. They see models of writing from authors, their teacher, and their peers throughout the process.

- Each day the students will have a chance to talk to one another whether it is formally as part of the days lesson (peer review, peer edit) or informally as discussed in chapter one (see Figure 1.4, The Role of Talk in Writing). And though talk will take place at different times in the lesson, I encourage you to give students a chance to incorporate the suggestions made by their peers just after the peer interaction.

- Scaffolding the draft by focusing students on one section at a time helps break down the discourse structure of narrative text. With attention to the generalizations of narratives as seen through Gary Soto's stories, ELs learn "how" to write narratives in English. Teachers are explicitly teaching about the discourse of English narrative writing throughout the development of the draft. Taking it one step at a time can reduce ELs' writing anxiety.

- The instructional writing sequence did not follow a linear writing process because it is truly an iterative and cyclical process. The students jump from drafting one day to revising, back to drafting, additional revising, some editing, some more drafting, and ultimately continuing their own process to complete their narrative. For example, after writing their beginnings the teacher engaged in some editing. This helps students then apply their new knowledge as they continue to write the rest of their story.

- At any point in the writing sequence you can use peer editing and revision with a focus on particular mini-lessons. For example, if you have been working on the use of prepositional phrases, have students engage in a peer revision session around prepositional phrases.

I am often asked how long the entire writing sequence takes. This question is always a difficult one to answer because any plan depends on the students. Each lesson can take a day or if necessary can take a couple of days before moving on. In some cases you might find yourself leaving parts out because your group of students does not need the heavy structure and support. What I have found useful is having a highly structured plan in place the first time you are writing narratives with your students. As students begin to develop independence as second language writers, you will not need to structure and scaffold their writing as much. Each time you come back to writing narrative text, release some of the responsibility to the students. You might choose to give them their own time for drafting and guide them through deeper, more complex revision and editing. Or, perhaps you continue to scaffold the draft but allow them the flexibility to engage in peer revision and editing as needed. Your decisions will come from what you see your students doing as writers. In addition, I like to provide students with a rubric that highlights what we have learned as writers. Figure 2.5, Personal Narrative Rubric, is a sample I have used for evaluating my students' personal narratives.

	4	**3**	**2**	**1**
ORGANIZATION	THERE IS A LOGICAL SEQUENCE OF EVENTS, INCLUDING A CLEAR BEGINNING, MIDDLE, AND END.	THERE IS A LOGICAL SEQUENCE OF EVENTS, INCLUDING A BEGINNING, MIDDLE, AND END.	THERE IS A LACK OF A CLEAR SEQUENCE OF EVENTS FROM BEGINNING TO END.	THE ORDER OF EVENTS IS CONFUSING. THERE IS NO CLEAR BEGINNING LEADING TO AN END.
ELEMENTS OF NARRATION	CONTAINS MANY DETAILS ABOUT THE SETTING, PEOPLE, AND EVENTS.	CONTAINS SOME DETAILS ABOUT SETTING, PEOPLE, AND EVENTS.	CONTAINS FEW DETAILS ABOUT SETTING, PEOPLE, AND EVENTS.	LACKS DETAILS ABOUT SETTING, PEOPLE, AND EVENTS.
	CONSISTENTLY WRITTEN IN FIRST PERSON POINT OF VIEW.	FREQUENTLY USES THE FIRST PERSON POINT OF VIEW.	POINT OF VIEW SHIFTS SOMETIMES IN THE ESSAY.	POINT OF VIEW SHIFTS THROUGHOUT THE ESSAY.
GRAMMAR, USAGE, MECHANICS, AND SPELLING	FIRST PERSON PRONOUNS ARE USED CORRECTLY.	THERE ARE SOME ERRORS IN THE USE OF FIRST PERSON PRONOUNS.	THERE ARE MANY ERRORS IN THE USE OF FIRST PERSON PRONOUNS.	FIRST PERSON PRONOUNS ARE USED INCORRECTLY THROUGHOUT.
	DIALOGUE IS PUNCTUATED PROPERLY THROUGHOUT.	FEW ERRORS IN PUNCTUATING DIALOGUE.	DIALOGUE IS RARELY PUNCTUATED PROPERLY.	DIALOGUE IS NOT PUNCTUATED PROPERLY.
	THERE ARE LITTLE TO NO ERRORS IN GRAMMAR, USAGE, AND MECHANICS.	THERE SOME GRAMMAR, USAGE, AND MECHANICS ERRORS.	THERE ARE SEVERAL ERRORS IN GRAMMAR, USAGE, AND MECHANICS.	THERE ARE NUMEROUS ERRORS IN GRAMMAR, USAGE, AND MECHANICS.

Figure 2.5 Personal Narrative Rubric

Source: used with permission from Katie Figueroa.

Figure 2.6 is an example of a Spanish-speaking third grader's personal narrative as a result of the instructional sequence above. At the time, she was at a speech emergent level of second language acquisition. This was her first draft. You will notice that her writing still contains some errors, mainly syntactic errors in sentence construction, but it is a strong beginning with a solid narrative structure. She uses transition words as a result of an early revision lesson on narrative transitions and attempted dialogue. With the discourse structure in place, from this point on the teacher can focus on elaborating her story and adding more descriptive language.

NARRATIVE GENRES

A variety of genres fit within the text type of narratives. Students will be familiar with the many genres within narrative writing because they are the kinds of stories they have been exposed to since infancy. Sometimes they are read to by their parents, often fictional narratives such as fairy tales, and they hear oral

Raquel

I went to Disnyland It all happened when I was four years old on a sunny day and I was bored and had nothing to do. My tia said "Were going to Disnyland!" and I was amazed.

Then I was getting ready to go in the car but I said, "Wait!" because I was going to say to my cousin that you want to come and he said, "Yes!" and we got in the car and drove to Disnyland.

Figure 2.6   Raquel's Personal Narrative (First Draft)   *(Continued)*

(Continued)

After a while I was
jumping crazy because I was
so excited because I was getting
in line for my first ride
Suddenly I was first in
line and the ride I went was
DaryanaJones and my tia and my
cousin went with me on the ride
and it had lava and it is fast
and the lava was hot and I
got on the ride and it was
scary.
Finally we went on some more

on the ride and then we bought stuff and we got in the car and left.

At last I got home and I was so excited because I wanted to play my things and my mom was so happy because my tia said "He has been a good boy," and I went to sleep with my sister.

stories from their families such as personal narratives, biographies, folklore, and tall tales. In addition to written and oral stories, children experience highly visual and multimedia narratives through movies and cartoons. By the time students begin school and are asked to formally write a narrative, they have been immersed in narrative genres. And though ELs come with a wealth of information and exposure to narrative genres, they will need guidance as to how they are written *in English*.

We will explore the generalizations and organization of three popular narrative genres, fairy tales, tall tales, and myths, children are required to write as part of most language arts curriculums. For additional narrative genres see Figure 2.7, Narrative Writing Genres.

Family history	Recount an observed event	Myths
Personal narratives	Tall tales	Monologues
Retelling of a story	Memoirs	Folktales
Diaries	Legends	Fables
Fantasy	Historical fiction	Screenplays
Narrative poems	Picture books	Science fiction

Figure 2.7 Narrative Writing Genres

Fairy Tales

Fairy tales are fictional tales with magical elements. They began as folktales passed on through oral tradition within and across ethnic cultures. They contain the most magical and extraordinary characters and elements. We are introduced to fanciful and fantastic characters such as talking animals, mermaids, and a wolf with the strength of a bulldozer. Children enjoy fairy tales because there is no limit to what a character can say and do. The enjoyment children experience when reading and watching fairy tales transfers to their work as writers of fairy tales. When children begin to explore and develop their ideas for a fairy tale, their minds begin to work in wonderful ways. They will think in the most creative ways as they try and develop characters and plots that will excite their audience. Fairy tales are emotional; they make you laugh and cry, cringe and shout, all within a short period of time.

When preparing students to write their own fairy tales, just as with any other writing task, they should have opportunities to read and explore the genre. Though fairy tales may differ in many ways, they normally contain the following elements:

- Foundations lie in oral traditions with stories of long ago.
- They begin with an enticing opening such as, "Once upon a time."
- There is a presence of magic.

- Royalty, animals, and/or peasants are used as main characters.
- Things often happen in threes or sevens.
- A battle, literally or figuratively, of good versus evil (hero vs. villain) takes place.
- Themes of love, kindness, and the value of goodness in people are common.
- Truth prevails over deception and lies.
- Have a happy ending.

Resource E: Looking Closely at a Fairy Tale and Resource F: Comparing Fairy Tales can help you work with your students to understand the elements of fairy tales. It can also be used when students plan their own stories. Resource G: Planning for Writing provides an additional organizer for planning a fairy tale. All of these graphic organizers and planners help expose ELs to the content and discourse of fairy tales. Taking the time to immerse ELs in fairy tales makes writing them less intimidating. You can also enhance your study of fairy tales by:

- Inviting family members to share fairy tales from their ethnic cultures.
- Allow students to come to school dressed as their favorite character from a fairy tale during an author celebration.
- Host a fairy tale ball, with refreshments, music, and dancing.
- In small groups select a fairy tale written by one group member to act out for the class.
- Create a movie poster for their fairy tale to present with their story.
- For older students you can also:
  o Create an iMovie movie preview (trailer) of their fairy tale.
  o Create a Power Point presentation of their fairy tale, similar to turning the pages of a book as they read through their fairy tale.
  o Make a mini-movie of a selected, original fairy tale in small groups.

As you plan for writing fairy tales with your students, be sure to scaffold the draft with attention to discourse. An instructional sequence similar to the one described for developing a personal narrative can be used for writing fairy tales. Students need to *see* how fairy tales are organized to remain true to the genre. Figure 2.8 is one of my second grader's fairy tales as a result of scaffolding the structure and elements of fairy tales. At the time he wrote this piece he was tested at an "early production" level of second language acquisition. You can see that the content of his fairy tale was inspired by a traditional fairy tale, The Gingerbread Man. This piece is his final draft.

Tall Tales

Another type of folk literature shared throughout history is tall tales. Tall tales are stories of creative solutions to our everyday challenges by larger-than-life characters. They allow students a chance to put into writing those quirky ideas we know they all have when going about their daily lives and thinking to themselves, "If only I could . . . I would . . . ." Children are

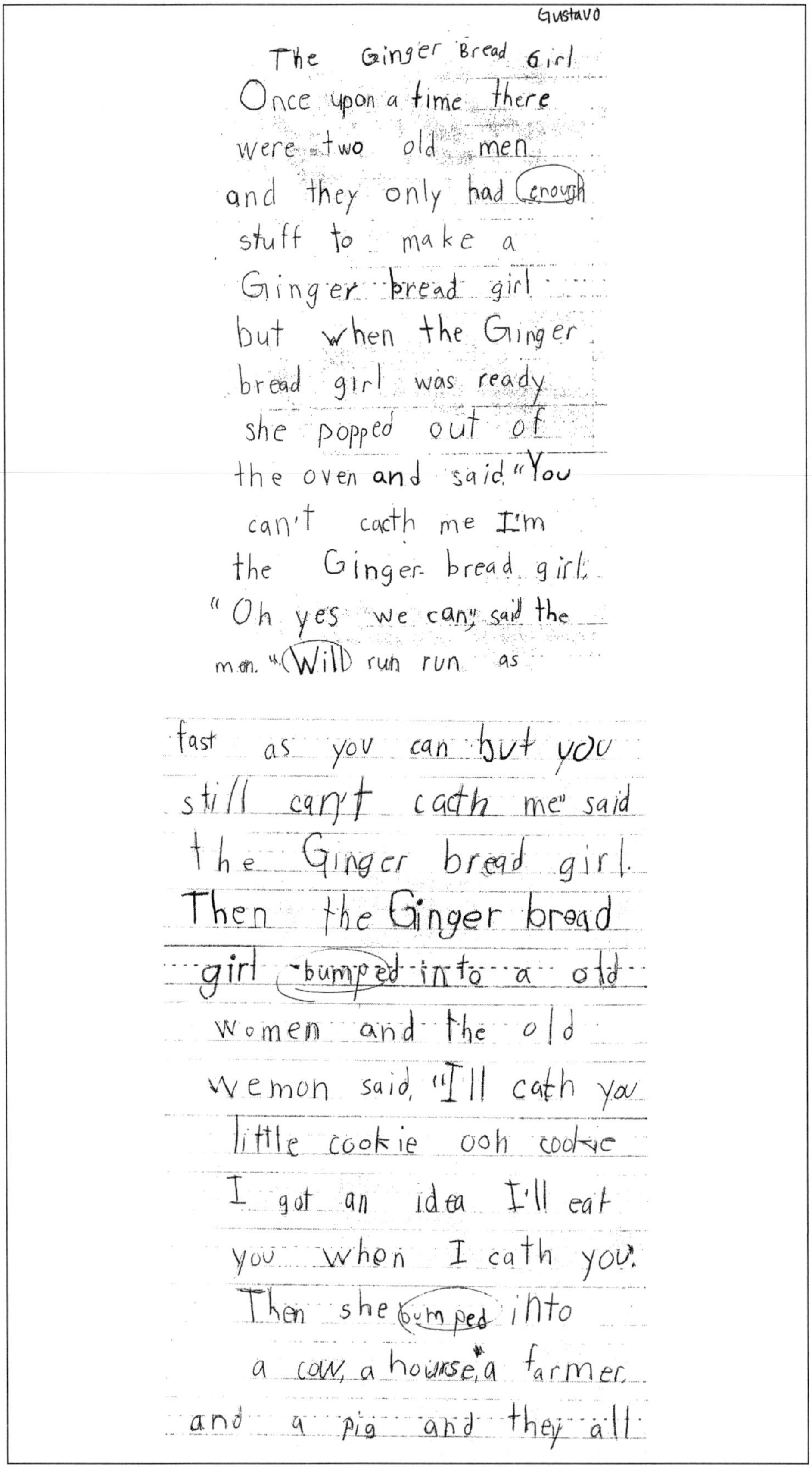

Gustavo

The Ginger Bread Girl
Once upon a time there
were two old men
and they only had (enough)
stuff to make a
Ginger bread girl
but when the Ginger
bread girl was ready
she popped out of
the oven and said "You
can't cacth me I'm
the Ginger bread girl.
"Oh yes we can" said the
men. "(Will) run run as

fast as you can but you
still can't cacth me" said
the Ginger bread girl.
Then the Ginger bread
girl bumped into a old
women and the old
wemon said, "I'll cath you
little cookie ooh cookie
I got an idea I'll eat
you when I cath you.
Then she bumped into
a cow, a hourse, a farmer
and a pig and they all

Figure 2.8   Gustavo's Fairy Tale

said," Well get you for that and the Ginger bread girl said," Oh well run run as fast as you can but you won't cact me"! And the Ginger bread girl ran and ran untill she came to a river and there she met a wolf and the Ginger bread girl said to the wolf hey wolf could

you give me a ride acros the river" And the wolf said (Shur) So the wolf gave the Ginger bread girl a ride but when they got to the other side the wolf ate the Ginger bread girl.

constantly thinking of ideas for tall tales as part of their inquisitive nature. All of their "what if?" stories, where they are 10 feet tall, can fly, or are strong enough to lift a car, are the ideas that drive tall tales. What we will do to help children bring about a full story from their "what if" statements is to guide them through the elements of a tall tale to capture their imaginary scenarios. The following are common elements of tall tales:

- There is an exaggeration about a characteristic or ability of the main character.
- The main character is an everyday person, using everyday language, with superhuman abilities.
- The setting is common for the problem, in a given time.
- The plot is funny and impossible in real life.
- The use of hyperbole, a figure of speech in which statements are exaggerated or extravagant, is common.
- Use a lot of action verbs and adjectives to show exaggeration.
- The problem is solved through the use of the main character's special superhuman characteristic.

When helping students think of ideas for tall tales, along with reading examples of tall tales, you want to help them realize that these stories come from their knowledge of familiar settings, of familiar problems in the world that can be solved in silly, extraordinary ways. Start by asking them to think of a series of problems they see as they are walking around their neighborhood, at the park, on a family trip, on the news, in the newspaper, or at home. Once they have identified some problems, ask them to think about how the problem can be solved in an unusual way. What would the main character have to do to solve the problem? What special characteristic would the main character need to solve the problem? Be sure to encourage risk taking with odd and impossible ideas for solving the problem so that students can be creative with their characters. These are the stories of superheroes!

To help guide your students in developing their tall tales, see Resource H: Planning for Writing—Tall Tales. Refer back to the instructional writing sequence on personal narratives when guiding students through their tall tales. Start by analyzing existing tall tales, allow them opportunities to list or quickwrite ideas for tall tales until they have collected a series of ideas, then have them use the graphic organizer to expand their ideas into tall tales. You can then carefully break down the draft, focusing on the development of one piece of the story at a time. This will help ELs stay true to the genre to ensure they have written a tall tale.

Myths

Myths introduce children to another type of folk literature. Though for some cultures myths are considered true stories, we will look at the genre of myths as fictional stories that help explain a natural phenomenon in a unique and imaginative way. Children will have a chance to explain how their world came to be. Myths are the stories that answer the age-old question of "why?".

They can be written about anything and everything. When I was teaching sixth grade, one of my students wrote his myth about why our blood is red. He came up with the most unusual and innovative way to explain a phenomenon that we just take as a fact, an "it is what it is." I always remember his topic choice because it was a perfect example that myths can creatively explain absolutely anything, even something as natural and scientific as the color of our blood.

Myths are the stories that explain the many things about our world that we take for granted. I remember another one of my sixth graders wrote a wonderful story about how the ocean became blue. It was the case of sibling rivalry. When Mother Nature's older sister got tired of her always copying everything she did and everything she liked, she decided to seek revenge. Mother Nature loved yellow and thought it was a great color for the ocean so that everyone could see all of the beautiful sea creatures. But when Mother Nature wasn't looking, her older sister changed it to blue so that no one could see what lied beneath. Then everyone would be angry at Mother Nature. And that is why the ocean is blue and not yellow. He concluded his myth by explaining the importance of being nice to your siblings.

Myths are a great way to capitalize on students' imagination. They will generate the most fascinating explanations for the most ordinary topics. And on occasion, as seen in the example of Mother Nature, myths can be taken further to teach a moral lesson.

When writing myths just as with many narratives, children have a chance to really let their imaginations run wild. What makes myths different and will motivate students is that it is a way for them to answer their own "why" questions. And we all know that they have a million "why" questions. We probably find ourselves playing with myths to entertain our children because of all of the "why" questions we get on a daily basis. Well, this is a chance for children to make up their own version of reality, their chance to play with nature.

In the case of myths, it is difficult to identify key elements because it is only limited by the students' imagination. There are no common settings, characters can be anyone, and there is not always a problem with a solution, just a unique way of answering "why" something has come to be. Resource I: Planning for Writing—Myths can help students begin to think about how they can approach the explanation of their chosen phenomenon.

MAKING IT PUBLIC

Where children are asked to write a variety of narrative topics and genres, they are not always provided opportunities to publish their work in more authentic ways. Typically, whether they are writing a fantasy or fable the finished product is in essay format. What excites children about writing is when they can take their ideas and "show them off" in more creative, authentic ways. "When students do not value writing or a specific writing task, they may exert as little effort as possible to complete it . . . One way to avoid such apathy is to involve students in writing activities that are authentic and aimed at a real audience" (Graham & Harris, 1997, p. 124). Figure 2.9, Publishing Narratives, provides some ideas for students to publish their narratives in ways that will inspire them to want to write.

Writing task	Ways to publish
PERSONAL NARRATIVE	MAKE A PICTURE BOOK
	MAKE A SCRAPBOOK OF THE EVENT
RECOUNT OF AN EVENT	BROADCAST NEWS STORY
	FEATURE ARTICLE IN A CLASS NEWSPAPER
NARRATIVE POEM	POETRY READING
	SUBMIT ONE FOR PUBLICATION TO A MAGAZINE OR POETRY CONTEST
	POETRY ANTHOLOGY
SCREENPLAYS	PUT ON A PLAY, ACT THEM OUT!
	WRITE A COMIC STRIP
	MAKE AN iMOVIE
	MAKE A MOVIE TRAILER
STORIES	CREATE A BOOK JACKET (USE A CEREAL BOX)
	MAKE A BOOK

Figure 2.9   Publishing Narratives

The suggestions above are not an exhaustive list, but I hope it helps you begin to think about different ways to let your students share their stories with others. I understand that we want students to know how to write traditional narrative essays because our accountability measures require it. So after the students have completed their revised and edited drafts of the narrative essay, instead of having them recopy it neatly for publication, give them a chance to turn it into something more creative. We want to bring the novel, the enjoyable, into our toughest subjects. Writing is no small feat for anyone, and so we want to make it something children will *want* to do, not *have* to do.

CONCLUSION

Narrative writing comes from our life experiences. All children have ideas for writing narratives because they have all had opportunities to experience life. What we need to remember, however, is that though ELs are full of ideas, they may not possess enough academic language to know how to structure their ideas into a coherent, well-crafted narrative *in English*. Our job as teachers is to take the time and analyze the structure and generalities of narratives to help ELs understand and learn how to write them. By scaffolding the structure of narratives with students, specifically at the drafting stage, children will better understand how to write their stories. Whatever the narrative topic might be, you need to take time to analyze the structure of the narrative with your students. This is best accomplished by sharing books with children that they can read as writers and modeling original narratives. Helping students learn to *see* the writing of texts will vicariously teach them to become better writers when they read independently.

RESOURCES FOR TEACHING NARRATIVE WRITING

Fairy Tales, Fables, Legends, and Myths: Using Folk Literature in Your Classroom (2nd edition), Bette Bosma

Narrative Writing: Learning a New Model for Teaching, George Hillocks Jr.

Writing Fiction for Children: Stories Only You Can Tell, Judy K. Morris

Narrative Picture Books (second through third grade)

Abuela, Arthur Dorros

Bedhead, Margie Palatini

A Chair for My Mother, Vera B. Williams

Elizabeti's Doll, Stephanie Stuve-Bodeen

The Keeping Quilt, Patricia Polacco

The Pain and the Great One, Judy Blume

The Relatives Came, Cynthia Rylant

Too Many Tamales, Gary Soto

Two Mrs. Gibsons, Toyomi Igus

Narrative Texts (fourth through eighth grade)

Any Small Goodness: A Novel of the Barrio, Tony Johnston

Becoming Naomi Leon, Pam Munoz Ryan

Blubber, Judy Blume

The Cay, Theodore Taylor

Crash, Jerry Spinelli

Esperanza Rising, Pam Munoz Ryan

Island of the Blue Dolphins, Scott O'Dell

Jacob Have I Loved, Katherine Paterson

The Janitor's Boy, Andrew Clements

Kira-Kira, Cynthia Kadohata

The Lion, the Witch and the Wardrobe, C.S. Lewis

Milkweed, Jerry Spinelli

There's a Boy in the Girls' Bathroom, Louis Sachar

Short Stories

Baseball in April and Other Stories, Gary Soto

Living Up the Street, Gary Soto

Local News: Stories, Gary Soto

Fairy Tales

Beauty (a mix of fairy tales), Sheri Tepper

A Frog Prince, Alix Berenzy

The Frog Prince, Continued, Jon Scieszka

Hansel and Gretel/The Witch's Story, Sheila Black

Jack and the Beanstalk, and The Beanstalk Incident (the giant's version), Tim Paulson

The Magic Circle (Hansel and Gretel from the witch's point of view), Donna Jo Napoli

The Paper Bag Princess, Robert N. Munsch

The Three Billy Goats Gruff, Janet Stevens

The Three Little Pigs

The Fourth Little Pig, Teresa Celsi

The Three Little Cajun Pigs, Berthe Amoss

Three Little Javelinas, Susan Lowell

Three Little Pigs, Jean Claverie

Three Little Pigs and the Big Bad Wolf, Glen Rounds

The Three Little Wolves and the Big Bad Pig, Eugene Trivizas

The Three Pigs, David Wiesner

The True Story of the Three Little Pigs, Jon Scieszka

Goldilocks and the Three Bears

Goldilocks and Little Bear's Birthday, Doug Renahan

Goldilocks and the Three Bears, Candice F. Ransom

Goldilocks Returns, Lisa Campbell Ernst

Little Red Riding Hood

Carmine: A Little More Red, Melissa Sweet

Little Red Riding Hood (Caldecott Honor Book), adapted by Trina Schart Hyman

Little Red Riding Hood: A Newfangled Prairie Tale (modernized), Lisa Campbell Ernst

Lon Po Po: A Red-Riding Hood Story from China, Ed Young (translator)

Red Riding Hood: The Brothers Grimm, Wilhelm Carl Grimm, Jacob Ludwig Carl Grimm

The Wolf's Story: What Really Happened to Little Red Riding Hood, Toby Forward

Cinderella

"Aschenputtel" or "Ash Girl," *Grimm's Household Tales*, Wilhelm Carl Grimm, Jacob Ludwig Carl Grimm

Cendrillon: A Caribbean Cinderella, Robert D. San Souci

Cinder Edna, Ellen Jackson

Cinderella and Cinderella: The Untold Story (stepsisters' perspective), Russell Shorto

Cinderella Bigfoot (Happily Ever Laughter), Mike Thaler and Jared Lee
Cinderella Penguin: Little Glass Flipper, Janet Perlman
Cinderella/That Awful Cinderella, Alvin Granowsky
Cinder-Elly, Frances Minters
Dinorella: A Prehistoric Fairy Tale, Pamela Duncan Edwards and Henry Cole
The Egyptian Cinderella, Shirley Climo
The Irish Cinderlad, Shirley Climo
The Korean Cinderella, Shirley Climo
Mufaro's Beautiful Daughters, John Steptoe
Persian Cinderella, Shirley Climo
Prince Cinders, Babette Cole
The Rough-Face Girl (the Algonquin Indians of North America), Rafe Martin
Slender Ella and Her Fairy Hogfather, by Vivian Sathre
Smoky Mountain Rose: An Appalachian Cinderella, Alan Schroeder
Sootface (an Ojibwa Cinderella story), Robert D. San Souci
Tattercoats, Margaret Greaves and Margaret Chamberlain
The Turkey Girl: A Zuni Cinderella Story, Penny Pollock
Yeh-Shen: A Cinderella Story from China, Ai-Ling Louie

Tall Tales

American Tall Tales, Adrien Stoutenburg
American Tall Tales, Mary Pope Osborne
Dona Flor: A Tall Tale about a Giant Woman with a Great Big Heart, Pat Mora
Here Comes McBroom!: Three More Tall Tales, Sid Fleischman
Johnny Appleseed: A Tall Tale, Steven Kellogg
Mike Fink, Steven Kellogg
Paul Bunyan, Steven Kellogg
Pecos Bill, Steven Kellogg

Myths

Bones in the Basket, C.J. Taylor
Favorite Greek Myths, retold by Mary Pope Osborne
The First Red Maple Leaf, Ludmila Zeman
How Two-Feather Was Saved from Loneliness, C.J. Taylor
How We Saw the World, C.J. Taylor
Sky Dragons and Flaming Swords: the Story of Eclipses, Comets, and Other Strange Happenings in the Skies, Marietta D. Moskin
Why Mosquitoes Buzz in People's Ears: A West African Tale, Verna Aardema

3 Expository Writing

Photo by Eugenia Mora-Flores.

*O*ne of the worlds' most fascinating animals is the dolphin. Dolphins are mammals that live in the ocean. They can grow between four to thirty feet long. They are very playful, look friendly and are one of the most intelligent animals. What makes dolphins so interesting is their playful behavior, eating habits, and how people hurt them.

Dolphins are a lot like kids because they love to play all day. They play fight with one another, bother sea birds, and even enjoy riding the waves. Oceanographers still don't know why but dolphins jump up out of the water doing flips sometimes. They think maybe they are looking down at the water at schools of fish to eat. Dolphins are very social. They live in pods with other dolphins and you can usually see them swimming and playing together. In areas where there is enough food available, you can find up to a thousand dolphins in a pod. They call this a superpod. These pods help one another during feedings.

Like a team, dolphins work together when it is time to eat. They will make a circle around a school of fish, taking turns eating. Except for the Orca they mainly eat squid and fish. The Orca also eats other marine mammals and will sometimes attack seals on the beach.

Dolphins are not an endangered species, but we still need to help save them because humans are responsible for many dolphin deaths. When we throw our trash in the ocean many dolphins eat the trash and get sick. Dolphins also run into boats or get caught in the propeller of the boat and are killed. Sometimes the dolphins get caught in the tuna fish nets and die. Lots of dolphins die every year because of the fisherman's boats. But, since people like to eat tuna and other fish I know we can't get rid of the fishermen. However, maybe there is a way for fisherman to be more careful about how they encounter dolphins in the ocean. In addition, everyone can help the dolphins by not polluting our beaches. Throw your trash away in the trash can because you can save a dolphin.

Dolphins are mammals that like to play with each other. They work together to eat and they need to be careful of fisherman's boats. If we take better care of our beaches we can help protect the dolphins.

—Marisol Mora (age eight), 2005

UNDERSTANDING EXPOSITORY WRITING

Extra, extra, read all about it! Expository writing is when children get to share information they know or have learned. The challenge in writing exposition is in the facts. Because it is based on real information, children need the background knowledge to write nonfiction. The piece above was written by my niece, Marisol, when she was in third grade. She was extremely motivated to work on this piece because dolphins are her favorite animal. She spent hours reading books and surfing the Internet researching dolphins. She printed out pages and pages of information, highlighting important information and taking notes along the way. As Marisol read through books she would write down information on sticky notes or index cards. Once she read through it all she decided on four main topics she wanted to cover in her paper; behavior, eating habits, human impact on dolphins, and notable facts. She then started making four separate piles of information based on her four topics. It was simply a matter of sorting her stick notes and printouts into the right pile. She then sifted through each pile one at a time, removing documents she was not going to use and putting the others in a logical order. Once her piles were in order, Marisol wrote out a bibliography of all the resources she planned on using. She then began to fill out a graphic organizer to plot out her ideas (see Resource J: Idea Map). Once this was finished she began to write out a first draft.

I point out her process because it is the work of expository writing. We spend days with our students finding a passion to explore and gathering all of the information needed to write about it. The purpose of expository writing is to inform, explain, clarify, define, or instruct and is often characterized by the following:

- Commitment to a topic
- Answers a key question about the topic
- Identifies subtopics for discussion
- Based on formal research, personal experience, or observation
- Provides information about the topic using examples, details, facts, comparisons, quotes from reputable sources, or relevant anecdotes
- Information is organized logically
- Usually written in the third person
- Written with the assumption that the information is new to the reader
- Vocabulary and unfamiliar concepts are well defined

I always enjoy working through expository writing with my students because they become so intrigued by what they are learning. You hear inquisitive voices saying, "I never knew that," "That's pretty cool," "I wonder why," and they share all they are learning with their friends and family. They feel empowered when they become the expert on a self-selected topic. But to generate interest and passion, students need choice. I remember when I was working on my doctoral dissertation my professor kept insisting that we select a topic we were passionate about. This was the best piece of advice I could have received. My interest in the topic made the research and writing bearable and even enjoyable. This is what we want for our students. We want them to be so invested in their research that they forget it is an assignment and they dive into learning. I do understand that in our work as teachers, choice often comes with limits. As a sixth grade humanities teacher, my students had to write about American history. I knew I couldn't have them just write about anything they wanted because our writing was embedded in our content area. But there was still room for choice. For example, when studying the American Revolution, the students were given choice in what they wanted to research. They could research anything that was going on in history at the time of the American Revolution. One student wrote about the changing demographics of America from a Native American perspective. Another student chose to research what was happening in the West at the time of the American Revolution. We need to find ways of broadening the writing task or prompt students are required to complete to give them choice. When we do they become more invested in their learning.

One of my favorite resources for teaching expository writing is *Nonfiction Matters* by Stephanie Harvey. This book really opened my eyes to what an expository genre study is really all about. I learned that it is the planning and research that precedes the writing of an expository piece that matters most. We need to give students time to gather the information they will need to write a great piece. Once they have the information, they can craft their expository essays in a variety of ways. Figure 3.1, Mini-Lessons for Preparing Writers for Exposition, introduces a variety of prewriting mini-lessons for preparing writers for exposition. Many of those included I learned from Stephanie Harvey while

- Self-selecting an interesting topic
- Generating research questions
- Identifying resources
- Locating information: Keeping a running bibliography
- Notetaking
- Retelling information versus plagiarism
- Paraphrasing
- Side bars (writing in the margins) for noting key ideas, themes, and questions. If students cannot write in the margins, you can use sticky notes for side bars.
- Highlighting key ideas
- Using an index
- Skimming text
- Surfing the Internet (validating references and information)

Figure 3.1 Mini-Lessons for Preparing Writers for Exposition

others I have created and adapted through my work with children. In addition, some of the resources I use to guide students research are included in Resource K: Collecting Data.

Once the students have gathered all of their information, they need further guidance on how to sift through it to determine what is relevant and useful. This leads to the use of graphic organizers (see Resource L: Organizing Information) to make logical sense of all of their information.

Just as with narrative writing, ideas for exposition come from our experiences. And through those experiences comes curiosity—a curiosity to learn more about something. We begin to ask questions and want to find the answers to those questions. This is the beginning of research. Once all the information has been collected we turn toward exploring the best way to represent that information to share it with others.

EXPOSITORY ESSAYS

Expository essays can take on a variety of organizational forms, including but not limited to description, time order, cause and effect, problem-solution, and compare and contrast. These five ways of organizing information are considered nonfiction text structures. Examples of these text structures can be found in the textbooks and trade books students are asked to read across the content areas. Figure 3.2, Expository Text Structures, provides more information on nonfiction text structures.

The organizational (discourse) structure of an expository essay often follows a logical presentation of ideas. Students need support in sifting through all of the information gathered for expository writing to present a coherent flow of information. Typically, students are asked to follow a traditional essay model when writing exposition. Figure 3.3, Expository (Discourse) Structure, provides a general structure for writing expository essays. This structure will need to be explicitly taught to English learners (ELs) to continue to build their written academic language. English learners need to understand how to write to inform, different from what they learned about narrative writing.

Pattern	Description	Cue Words
Description	The author describes a topic by listing characteristics, features, facts, and examples. Author calls attention to sensory detail, awareness of audience, and perspective.	For example, Characteristics include As an example For instance
Sequence	The author lists items or events in numerical or chronological order. Includes "how-to" reports.	First, second, third, next, then, finally Today, yesterday, tomorrow After, after a few days, after a short time, at last In conclusion, in closing, last of all In review
Comparison (compare/contrast)	The author explains how two or more things are alike and/or different.	Different In contrast Alike Same as Although Yet In much the same way On the other hand On the contrary Unlike Whereas
Cause and effect	The author lists one or more causes and the resulting effect(s). A relationship in which one thing may have a resulting effect on another.	Reasons why If . . . then Accordingly As a result For this reason On account of Since . . . therefore Therefore Because
Problem/solution	The author states a problem and lists one or more solutions for the problem. An analysis of a complex situation or problem. Also referred to as question/answer in which the author poses a question and then answers it.	Problem is Dilemma is Puzzle is solved Question . . . answer In effect As a result (of) On account of A case in point Although it is true

Figure 3.2 Expository Text Structures

Introduction		Body		Conclusion
Presentation of topic	Thesis	Supporting paragraphs	Transitions	Restatement
1. Introduction of the topic 2. Define the topic in the context of your paper	What will be the focus of your paper? What about the topic will you write about?	1. Maintain topic/thesis 2. Factual information 3. Examples 4. Quotes	To connect one paragraph to another Maintains logical sequence	Restate the thesis or topic and main ideas Do not introduce new material

Figure 3.3 Expository (Discourse) Structure

In addition to how the actual text is organized, we also need to share with students other features of nonfiction text, including:

- Table of contents
- Headings and subheadings
- Use of graphs, tables, maps, and charts
- Use of real pictures
- Questioning techniques within the text, and
- Bibliographies

We often teach these elements of nonfiction as a way to facilitate comprehension of content area texts and when teaching students how to research information. I further encourage teachers to show students how to use these features of nonfiction texts in their own expository writing. Think about your academic writing and how headings and subheadings help you organize your ideas. We should encourage the same of our students. The expository essay does not have to limit itself to just text. Figure 3.4, "The Physical State of the Nation," is an excerpt from one of my undergraduate student's papers for an independent study course. What I want you to focus on as you read her text is how effectively she uses headings, graphs, charts, and even a cartoon to support her writing. Expository writing should come to life through its many unique elements. This can be expected of our children and adolescents as well. The sample in Figure 3.5, "Save the Planet," was created by Rocio, a seventh grader, during a study on environmental issues. Using Brittani's piece as a model for writing, Rocio found ways of incorporating features of nonfiction text in her own writing. This is a great way for ELs to demonstrate their learning through varied written forms. The amount of text ELs are required to process in a second language when researching can become overwhelming. Seeing the content to be learned through cartoons, graphs, charts, illustrations, pictures, and logos enhances their comprehension of the material. In turn they can then use the same varied forms of written text to share their learning within a traditional expository essay.

THE PHYSICAL STATE OF THE NATION

Earlier this semester, when I was waiting for the tram and thinking about what I should write about, I noticed an ad on the side of a bus, or more like a warning that read *obesity in small children is a big problem.* This coupled with television commercials with young children asking their parents and loved ones for more cholesterol and diabetes followed by ads for "Big Mac's" and "Whoppers" made me realize that America's children are receiving mixed signals: they are not in shape and worse yet they are not healthy. According to the Center of Disease Control and Prevention website the prevalence of overweight children ages 2–5 has more than doubled from 5% to 13.9%, while 6–11 year-olds nearly tripled from 6.5% to 18.8% and those children from ages 12–19 rose significantly from 5% to 17.4% (2007). Obesity is a huge problem that has consequences including hyper tension, coronary heart disease, stroke, Type II diabetes, some cancers and the list goes on

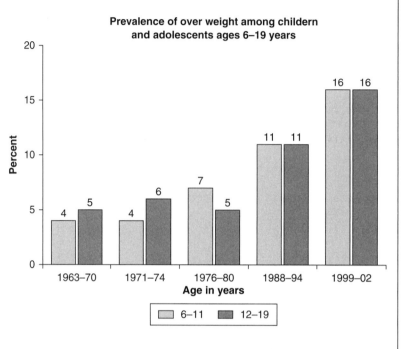

(CDC, 2007). Amidst, all of this however there is hope and it can begin in our schools. The Center for Disease control and Prevention argues that physical activity not only has beneficial effects on body weight but also improves blood pressure and bone strength. Even better is their finding that children who participate in physical activity are more likely to become adolescents and adults who participate in physical activity (CDC, 2007). Therefore, Physical Education can be the starting point of a healthy America.

NUTRITION AND EXERCISE

Healthy America begins in the classroom or in this instance outside of the classroom. Additionally, for quality physical education instruction to be effective students need to understand the importance of physical activity and nutrition, For this to occur, many changes need to be made in schools. For instance it is going to be difficult to convince students that they need to eat healthy when the campus is overrun with vending machines offering soft drinks, chips and candy bars. This comic strip also demonstrates how PE is perceived as a waste of time while it also depicts how lazy Americans have become. The school needs to take control of the situation and reevaluate their priorities. An example of this was demonstrated in the article, "Students' Perceptions of the Impact of Nutrition Policies on Dietary Behaviors," (2006) the researchers Stephanie Vecchiareli, Sumiko Takayanagi, and Charlotte Neuman did a study on how students felt about nutritional changes at two LAUSD high schools. Encouragingly 55% of students indicated that the policy impacted the beverages they drank at home, while similarly

"Oh - and can my Mum take me - around in her 4x4 - Sir?"

Figure 3.4 "The Physical State of the Nation" *(Continued)*

(Continued)

52.6% indicated that the policy on junk food changed their eating habits outside of school. These students made lifestyle changes based on policy changes that affected their school. What is also encouraging is that thirty-four states enacted similar legislation. However, not all students were affected some commented that it made them want more junk food at home. This is where there are problems with policy. Policy and legislation can only change so much on its own, individuals, such as teachers and administrators, need to create programs that talk about the positive benefits of eating healthy and exercising.

Physical educators can be used as a resource. Physical education is not simply running around the track for forty minutes, but can be used a tool to expand knowledge about nutrition Parents can also be used as a resource to healthy living in students, especially with primary students. Parents can encourage students to take control of their eating by allowing them to choose between carrots or celery, oranges or bananas, and they can make the easy switch to whole grain bread. These are simple changes that can go along way (McAllister, 2006, pg 46). However, awareness about nutrition and exercise are not enough. These strategies and ideas need to be put into place. The Journal of Pediatric Obesity reported that by 2010, "50% of children in North America will be overweight" (McAllister, 2006, pg 46) while according to the center for Disease control and prevention 45% of students grades 9–12 "are not engaged in sufficient physical activity or in physical activity at all" (as cited by Christie, 2005, pg 5–7). There appears to be a direct link between obesity and a lack of physical activity and Physical educators can turn that around.

PE EFFECTS ON STUDENTS

Attendance in physical education classes (based on five days per week) has dropped from 41% in 1991 to 28% in 2003 (as cited by Christie, 2005). Students are not getting the required physical activity they need and this makes perfect sense when PE and Art classes are always the first classes cut because of budget problems. PE can no longer be looked down upon as the "easy A" class but it should be regarded as essential for students. Physical education benefits students in a myriad of ways ranging from the development of physical skills, and "physical activity is associated with a longer and better quality of life, [and] reduced risk of a variety of diseases" (Bailey, 2006, pg 397–401). Physical education affects the physical domain as well as positively affects *lifestyle development, affective development, social development, and cognitive development.* According to researcher Richard Bailey in his article, "Physical Education and Sport in Schools" (2006) exclusion from physical education and sport is associated with inactivity which in turn is linked to obesity and a number of other health conditions. Bailey also asserts that students who are involved in regular physical activity and sports are less stressed out, depressed, or anxious which contributes to a psychologically healthy individual. Lastly, in the cognitive domain students who exercise and are active can experience cognitive advances. Working out "increases the flow of blood to the brain, enhancing mood, increasing mental alertness, and improving self-esteem" (Bailey, 2006, pg 397–401). What is also important to note was Bailey's citing of an

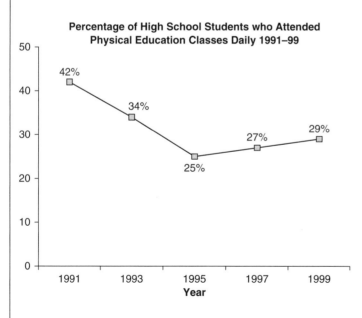

Percentage of High School Students who Attended Physical Education Classes Daily 1991–99

Save the Planet!

Could the world really be coming to an end? Sometimes I think it's true. We hear so much on the news telling us how much we are hurting the Earth. It makes me wonder if it's possible for people to really destroy the planet Earth. Sometimes I hear people say they don't care because they'll dead before it happens. But how can someone feel OK helping to destroy the Earth. I think we all need to do what we can to protect the Earth because it is not something we can replace. As kids we think there is not that much we can do because we don't drive yet and we don't pay bills. So when they say carpool or save energy with special light bulbs and windows. What can we do? But everybody, even kids can help save the plant. Kids can start a recycling program in their neighborhood, save energy at home, and volunteer in clean up programs.

Recycle

Recycling is one of the easiest ways to help save the planet. You can recycle soda cans, water bottles, paper and newspapers. It's so simple. Start by getting your trash cans ready. Pick two cans to label one cans/bottles and the other one paper. So your family won't get confused you can even write the recycling symbol on the cans. Then they will remember not to throw trash in the recycle cans. After the cans are full you can look for a recycling center in your neighborhood. A lot of recycling centers are in the parking lot of grocery stores. When you recycle you get paid for bottles and soda cans. You don't get money for recycling paper but you are saving the planet so you should recycle everything.

You can also organize a neighborhood recycling program. You can use the money you get from recycling and buy some big trash bags to pass out to your neighbors every week. Ask them to fill the bags with bottles, cans and paper. Then they can leave them outside for you to pick up. You can pick one day a week to tell them to put the bags outside so you can pick them up. This will make you a lot more money and then you know that more stuff is getting recycled.

April 1970 on Earth Day the recycling symbol was made by Gary Dean Anderson from USC who won a contest by the Container Cooperation of America

Save Energy at Home

www.aacog.com/archive/community/kidszone/kids. . .

Do you do this? When you leave the house do you sometimes leave the lights on and the TV? This is wasting energy. There are very easy way to save energy at your home. Start by turning off the lights every time you leave the room. If you have a TV turn it off when you leave the room too. You can also save energy by unplugging the blender and the toaster when no one is using it. Even if you don't use them because your mom and dad do the cooking, you can still look and see if they unplugged them. If they forgot, you can unplug them.

You can also help the planet when your at home when you save water. You should try and take short showers. Only take like 5 minutes. And when you brush your teeth turn off the water if you are brushing. Don't turn it back on until you have to wash out your mouth. All you have to do help save the planet from home is to pay attention to the lights and water. Turn them off!

Volunteer to Clean Up

The beaches are full of trash. This hurt our oceans. When people go to the beach they sometimes forget to throw away their trash. They leave it on the sand and when the water comes up it washes the trash into the ocean. When there is trash in the ocean two things can happen. The fish can get caught in the trash or they can eat the trash. The two things can kill the fish. You can help save the fish by volunteering in beach clean up days. You can look on the internet for the closest beach. You can mostly find beach clean up days in the summertime. There is a website on the internet called www.beachcleanup.org where you can find out about beach clean up days and how you can help.

Conclusion

Helping save the Earth is easy. Even kids to help out. Just start by recycling your soda cans and water bottles and turning off the lights at home when your not using them. Together we can save the fish in the ocean by volunteering in beach clean up days. If everyone does these three things our Earth will last a little bit longer.

Figure 3.5   "Save the Planet"

Aside from developing the background knowledge on their topic and understanding the different features of nonfiction text, an additional challenge for students is organizing their ideas coherently. They find so much information on their topic that they have a hard time compiling the facts into a cohesive text. They want to put in everything they've learned, which often leads to disjointed pieces of information. Careful planning for exposition is important to help students locate information, sift through research, and structure their text effectively. Teachers can support students in this process through the use of modeled and guided lessons on how to research. Students will need a couple of weeks, minimum, to gather information and organize it logically before beginning to write.

EXPOSITORY GENRES

National and state standards ask students to demonstrate competence in writing a variety of expository genres. Students are asked to begin by writing simple descriptive paragraphs to complex research reports and technical documents. Figure 3.6, Expectations for Expository Writing (Second Through Eighth Grade), provides a summary of California state and national standards related to exposition. Unlike narrative text, exposition lends itself nicely to an interdisciplinary approach. Expository writing is a great way to integrate writing throughout the curriculum. Students can write their paragraphs, compositions, and reports on any topic in science, social studies, music, art, physical education, and math. This is a wonderful opportunity to find more time in your school day for students to write! When I was teaching middle school, my students would write expository essays based on our history research. My second graders would write expository pieces on fossils, animal habitats, and astronomy. All of our hard work within the content areas is the groundwork, the background knowledge that leads to rich expository writing. For many of our students at the middle school level, expository writing happens in the content areas, while narrative writing and responses to literature are the focus in English class. But in all grade levels two through eight, there is room for exposition across all content areas.

Biographies

A popular expository genre students are asked to write in school is biographies. Figure 3.7, Instructional Writing Sequence for Biographies, provides a detailed sequence of lessons to prepare students for writing a biography. You will notice there is a great deal of research and preparation at the inception of the sequence that does not always include students writing drafts. Once all the necessary information has been collected and students understand what a written biography looks like, then a carefully scaffolded first draft is created. Just as with narrative writing, the key when teaching ELs to write exposition is to break down the discourse of the writing at the draft stage. This will lead to better first drafts and deeper revision and editing. The following instructional sequence has been used with a variety of classrooms ranging from third to eighth grade. The examples included in the sequence were generated in

(Text continued on page 60)

GENRE/STRUCTURE

CREATE A PARAGRAPH

CREATE A MULTIPLE-PARAGRAPH COMPOSITION

WRITE INFORMATION REPORTS

WRITE RESEARCH REPORTS

WRITE TRADITIONAL STRUCTURES, INCLUDING:

- CAUSE AND EFFECT
- COMPARE AND CONTRAST
- SEQUENCE
- PROBLEM-SOLUTION
- DESCRIPTIONS

WRITE DOCUMENTS RELATED TO CAREER DEVELOPMENT:

- BUSINESS LETTERS
- JOB APPLICATIONS
- MEMORANDUMS
- LETTER OF INQUIRY

WRITE TECHNICAL DOCUMENTS:

- IDENTIFY THE SEQUENCE OF ACTIVITIES NEEDED TO DESIGN A SYSTEM
- OPERATE A TOOL
- EXPLAIN THE BYLAWS OF AN ORGANIZATION

EXPOSITORY WRITING SKILLS

1. DEVELOP A TOPIC WITH SIMPLE FACTS, DETAILS, EXAMPLES, AND EXPLANATIONS
2. GROUP RELATED IDEAS
3. MAINTAIN A CONSISTENT FOCUS
4. PRESENT EVENTS IN SEQUENCE OR CHRONOLOGICAL ORDER
5. PROVIDE DETAILS AND TRANSITIONAL EXPRESSIONS THAT LINK ONE PARAGRAPH TO ANOTHER IN A CLEAR LINE OF THOUGHT
6. OFFER A CONCLUDING SUMMARY PARAGRAPH THAT SUMMARIZES IMPORTANT IDEAS AND DETAILS
7. FRAME QUESTIONS THAT DIRECT THE INVESTIGATION
8. STATE AND DEFINE A THESIS OR PURPOSE
9. OFFER PERSUASIVE EVIDENCE TO VALIDATE ARGUMENTS AND CONCLUSIONS
10. ENGAGE THE INTEREST OF THE READER AND STATE A CLEAR PURPOSE
11. USE STRATEGIES OF NOTETAKING, OUTLINING, AND SUMMARIZING TO IMPOSE STRUCTURE ON COMPOSITION DRAFTS
12. UNDERSTAND ORGANIZATION, PURPOSE, AND USE OF VARIOUS REFERENCE MATERIALS
13. QUOTE OR PARAPHRASE INFORMATION, CITE THEM BY MEANS OF FOOTNOTES AND/OR BIBLIOGRAPHY
14. DRAW FROM MORE THAN ONE SOURCE OF INFORMATION
15. USE A VARIETY OF PRIMARY AND SECONDARY SOURCES AND DISTINGUISH THE NATURE AND VALUE OF EACH
16. USE FORMATTING TECHNIQUES (E.G., HEADINGS, DIFFERING FONTS) TO AID COMPREHENSION
17. ORGANIZE AND DISPLAY INFORMATION ON CHARTS, MAPS, AND GRAPHS

Figure 3.6   Expectations for Expository Writing (Second Through Eighth Grade)

What Is a Biography?

Introduction: What is a biography? Using shared writing, students will provide any background knowledge on stories they have heard or read that tell about someone's life. The teacher will chart their responses.

Mini-lesson: **Understanding biographies.** Read *Lou Gehrig: The Luckiest Man* by David Adler (this is the picture book version of the story). After reading the story as a read-aloud, the teacher will orally model a retell of the biography she just read to the class.

Independent writing: The teacher will pass out short biographies for students to explore.

Share: Students will retell the biography they read to a partner (pair-share).

Exploring Biographies

Introduction: "Yesterday, we read examples of biographies. Today we are going to look at how they are written, what is included in a biography?"

Mini-lesson: **Understanding the content of a biography.** Read *Harvesting Hope: The Story of Cesar Chavez* by Kathleen Krull. Ask the students what information they noticed was included in the biography. The teacher posts on large chart paper the students' responses.

Independent writing: With a partner the students are provided a biography to explore. After reading the biography, they write down the type of information that was included. For example:

- Date of birth
- Birthplace
- Job
- Family
- Education
- Accomplishments
- Hardships
- Death

Share: Partnerships share out loud to the class what they discovered as the teacher records new ideas on the class chart created during the mini-lesson.

Gathering Information

Introduction: "You all came up with a great list of what is included in a biography. Today we are going to think about how to gather the information we need to write a biography." She explains that one way of learning about someone's life is by conducting an interview. But before interviewing someone, you need to think about which questions you will want to ask them.

Mini-lesson: **Generating questions to collect information.** The next step is gathering information about the life of their subject. Based on the responses from the previous day (see the class chart on elements of biography created the lesson before), students will begin to create an interview protocol. The teacher begins by modeling the first few questions. For example, on the chart the class had identified date of birth and job as two elements to include in a biography. "So if we wanted to find out when someone was born we would turn it in to a question. It would sound and look like this, "When were you born?" The teacher writes her question on a large chart paper titled, "Interview Protocol." She models another question, "What do you do for a living?"

Independent writing: Working with the same partners as the day before, the students revisit their list of "type of information included in a biography" and begin to generate a list of questions.

Share: Partnerships share out loud their questions, and they are added to the class "Interview Protocol" chart.

Figure 3.7   Instructional Writing Sequence for Biography   *(Continued)*

(Continued)

Selecting a Subject for the Biography

Introduction: Students will be provided CHOICE in selecting anyone they know as the subject for their biography. The teacher explains, "Today you are going to start thinking about who you might want to write about for your biography."

Mini-lesson: **Selecting an appropriate subject**. The teacher begins by modeling a list of people in her life that she may want to write about in her biography. Her list includes:

- My dad, Juan
- My mom, Maria
- My aunt, Feliza
- My uncle, Juvenal
- My aunt, Lucidia
- My boss, Mr. Baumann
- My friends, Vicki and Claudia
- The manager at Target

The teacher stops and asks the students to close their eyes and picture all the people they know in their families, at school, and in the community. In two to three minutes, students pair-share the people they pictured. (This will count as the share portion of the lesson.)

Independent writing: Students return to their seats and begin to generate a list of people they may want to write about for their biography.

Introduction: "We started to think about a variety of people for our biographies, and today we are going to start to narrow down who we are going to pick."

Mini-lesson: **Selecting a good subject for a biography**. The teacher brings forward their chart on "Elements of Biography" and her "List of Possible Subjects." Through a think-aloud the teacher demonstrates how to narrow down her choices. "So I am looking at my list of things to write about in a biography and I want to see which of my subjects I could find out a lot of this information from." The teacher places a star next to those subjects on her list whom she could find out a lot of information about various aspects of their lives. "Now I am thinking, since I will have to interview the person, I want to think about who would be accessible, easy to get a hold of for the interview." She places stars next to those subjects who are easily accessible. "Now I am thinking, whom do I just really want to know more about? Who would be interesting to talk to about their life?" She places a third star next to the people she is anxious to learn more about. "If I look at my list I notice that some of my names have one, two, or three stars. If I want to make sure I will have all of the information I need to write a biography, then I should pick someone with three stars." She looks at her three starred subject and circles three possibilities.

Independent writing: The students are then asked to return to their seats and take out their list of possible subjects for their biography. Through a guided practice model, the teacher asks students one question at a time as they place their stars next to their list of names. Once they have finished, they look at their possible subjects with three stars and circle their top choices.

Share: Students turn to their partner and tell them the three possibilities for their biography.

Conducting an Interview

Introduction: "Now that we have an idea of who we want to write about, let's look back at how we can gather the information we need to write the biography. You all came up with a list of questions that would give you the information you might want to include in your biography. I have typed them up for you and we will be using it to interview our subjects." (See the sample created by Mrs. Machado's third grade class Resource M: Interview Protocol.)

Mini-lesson: **Conducting an interview**. The teacher invites one student to come up and be her research subject. She then takes her interview protocol, sits face to face with the student, and begins her interview. "Hello Domingo, thank you again for agreeing to help me with my biography. I am really looking forward to hearing all about your life. If it's OK with you, I'd like to begin." The teacher begins to ask the questions and Domingo answers. When she asked, "What do you do for a living?" Domingo replied, "I go to school." "Could you tell me more about that; what exactly do you do at school?" The teacher continues the interview elaborating on questions to elicit more information from her subject. Once the interview is over the teacher will debrief with the class. "So what did you notice?" The class creates a chart entitled, "Conducting an Interview" to record their understanding of how to conduct an interview. For example, one student said, "You started with hello and that you were excited about learning about him." "OK so you are saying that we want to open the interview with a greeting." So as the students shared what they noticed, the teacher rephrased it for the chart. The class chart read:

- Start with a greeting
- Look at the person, pay attention with your eyes and ears
- Use the interview protocol to ask questions
- Ask follow-up questions if they don't give you a lot of information the first time.
- Ask other questions that are not on the interview protocol.
- Ask them if they have anything else they want to share openly.
- Thank them for their time and information.

Independent writing: With a partner the students are provided the interview protocol and practice interviewing each other.

Share: Students are asked to share out their successes and challenges in conducting their mock interviews.

Contacting Your Subject and Other Resources

Introduction: "Now that we are ready to begin our research, we need to discuss the proper protocols for conducting the interview, how we are going to contact the person." The teacher shares that they will want to let their subject know exactly what the interview is for and that they will share their biographies with them when completed.

Mini-lesson: **Accessing information about your subject.** Where else can we access information for writing a biography? She creates her own list of other resources for her subject, her dad, Juan Mora. Her list included:

- Ask his wife, my mom
- Look at his photo albums
- Talk with his other kids
- Look at any personal or family artifacts
- Ask his employees

Independent writing: The students are asked to create a personal list of where else they can find out information about their subject. This only takes about five minutes. They then have another five to ten minutes to ask their neighbors for help and add to their list.

Share: Students share out additional resources to add to the class list.

Homework: Students are asked to conduct their interviews and gather any other sources of information about their subject. This can be done in the preferred language of the student and subject.

Organizing Our Data

Introduction: "Last night you started conducting your interviews at home and looking for other information about your subject. Don't forget to bring it in with you tomorrow so we can start looking at how we will write it in a draft."

(Continued)

(Continued)

Mini-lesson: **Written discourse structure of biographies**. "Today we will look at some more biographies, but instead of focusing on what information is included, we will look closer at how it is written. Specifically, where the information is presented." The teacher goes back to the biography of Lou Gehrig that they read on day one. She reminds them of the information that was presented in the biography but begins to chart where the information was located in the story. She records on a large piece of butcher paper the information that was included at the beginning, middle, and end of the biography.

Beginning	Middle	End

Independent writing: With a partner the students are asked to complete a similar chart using sticky notes to document the information from the biography they were given to read. Figure 3.7a, Biography Sequence, is a sample of the students working on their chart.

Figure 3.7a   Biography Sequence

Share: The class shares out what they found. The teacher records what they found by rephrasing it to demonstrate what type of information they found at the beginning, middle, and end. Figure 3.7b, Sequencing Examples, is what was generated from the share out.

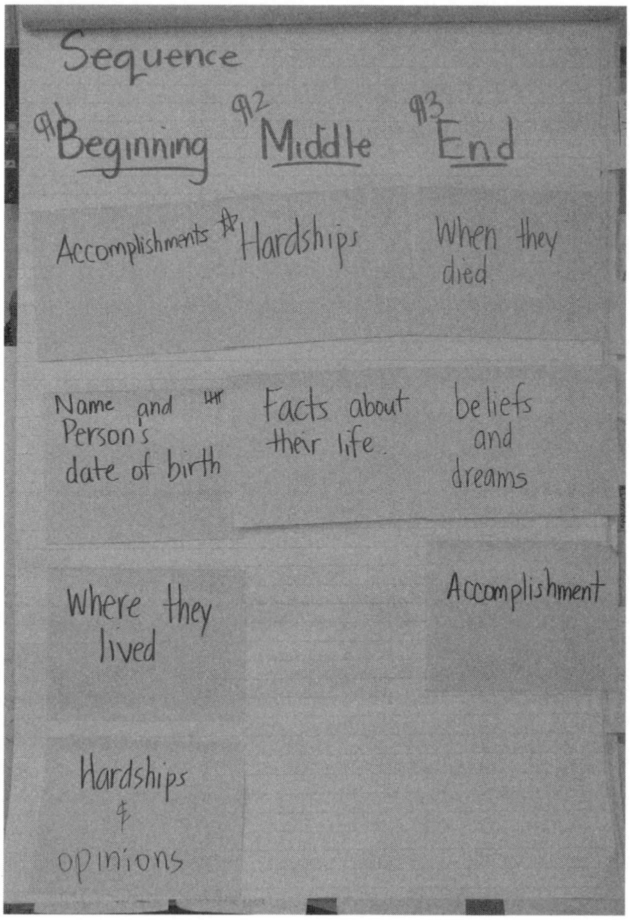

Figure 3.7b Sequencing Examples

Organizing Our Biographies

Introduction: "Now that we have explored how biographies are organized, we are ready to start planning our own biographies."

Mini-lesson: **Organizing information**. The teacher will use all of the information she has collected on her subject and model how to plan out their biographies by completing a "Beginning, Middle, End" chart for her own biography on her dad.

BEGINNING	MIDDLE	END
BORN ON AUGUST 22, 1946 BORN IN GUADALAJARA, JALISCO, MEXICO	LIVED ALONE IN TIJUANA LEARNED HOW TO FIX CARS OPENED HIS OWN AUTO MECHANIC SHOP MARRIED MARIA EUGENIA RUIZ HAD SIX CHILDREN	WORKS TIRELESSLY AS A MECHANIC HAS TEN GRANDCHILDREN ENJOYS SPENDING TIME WITH HIS FAMILY

(Continued)

(Continued)

Independent Writing: The students will complete their own "Beginning, Middle, End" chart for their own biographies.

Share: The teacher can call on three different students to share out loud topics included in the beginning, middle, and end of their biographies.

Drafting the Beginning

Introduction: "Today we'll use our data, all of the information we found about our subject, and begin to draft the beginning of our biography."

Mini-lesson: **Drafting the beginning.** The teacher looks back at her sequence of information chart about her dad and engages in a modeled writing to begin her draft.

Independent writing: The students are asked to draft their beginnings. If students finish early, they are encouraged to look back at their list of possible subjects and practice a beginning for another person. If they do not finish, that is OK; they will continue to work on it the following day.

Share: The students read their beginning paragraph(s) to their partner.

Improving Our Opening

Introduction: "We started our drafts yesterday, and I started thinking about ways we can improve our opening. We want to really show the audience that they just have to read this biography."

Mini-lesson: **Introducing a biography**. The teacher looks over the sequence work her students did with the sticky notes during the lesson on "organizing our data." She points out that they wrote different types of beginnings from the biographies they read. She notes, "Some of your biographies started with a quote, others with their birthdate. How else did you notice they started?" The class began to generate a list with examples in Figure 3.7c, The Beginning of a Biography.

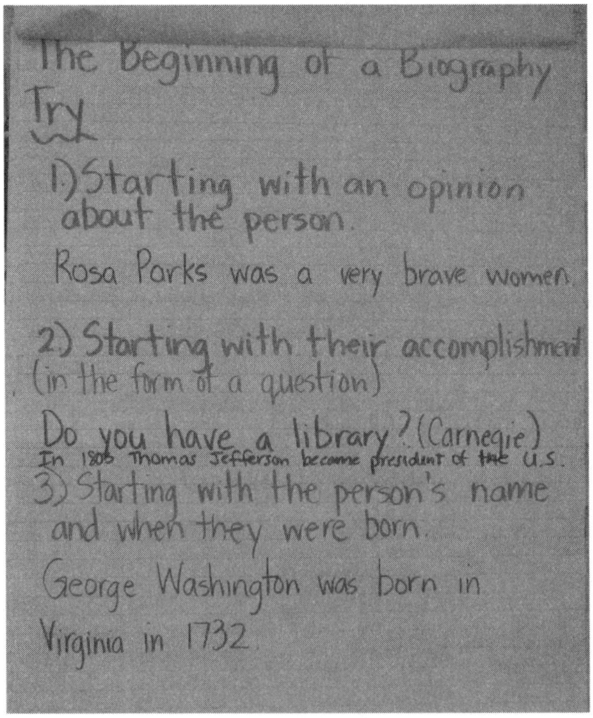

Figure 3.7c   The Beginning of a Biography

Independent writing: The students are asked to revisit the opening of their biography and create three different possible openings. Remember that at this point the students may not have finished their beginnings yet; they will be at different places but they will all, at the least, have an opening. So everyone can participate.

Share: They share their three possible openings and ask their partner for suggestions on which one sounds the best. Which one would make them want to read the biography?

Continuing the Draft (The Middle)

Introduction: "Today we will continue to write our drafts, finishing up the beginning and moving on to the middle."

Mini-lesson: **Drafting the middle**. The teacher begins by rereading what she has written thus far about her father. Then, looking back at the sequence of information chart about her dad, she models writing "the middle" of her biography about her dad.

Independent writing: The students are asked to continue to work on their beginnings and move on to the middle. If students finished early, they are encouraged to look back at their list of possible subjects and practice a beginning for another person and a middle. So some students will have multiple drafts they are working on, but their main draft is the one they conducted research on. If they do not finish, that is OK; they will continue to work on it the following day.

Share: The students read to a partner what they have added to their draft.

Continuing the Draft (The End)

Introduction: "Today we will continue to write our drafts, continuing to work on the beginning and middle but looking at the end now."

Mini-lesson: **Drafting the end.** Again the teacher will begin by rereading her entire biography to this point. She then revisits the sequence of information chart for what to talk about at the end of her biography. Using the information, she completes the end of her biography on her dad through modeled writing.

Independent writing: The students are asked to continue to work on their beginnings and middle and move on to the end. If students finished early, they are encouraged to look back at their list of possible subjects and practice a full draft of another subject. So some students will have multiple drafts they are working on, but their main draft is the one they conducted research on. If they do not finish, that is OK; they will continue to work on it the following day.

Share: The students read to a partner what they have added to their draft.

Focus on the Syntax and Discourse of Biographies

Introduction: "As we continue to draft, I want you to look at how you are organizing your information."

Mini-lesson: **Sequence and transitions**. The teacher uses a list of transition phrases that are common and useful for maintaining a logical sequence for a biography. They include:

- During the early years of their life . . .
- When _____ was a child . . .
- As he grew older . . .
- When he was a teenager . . .
- After his work as a _____
- After he _____ he became a_____
- As an adult . . .
- Later in life . . .

Independent writing: The students will look over their drafts and see if their transitions are helping to maintain the sequence of the person's life. They can use the frames provided or some of their own.

Share: The teacher selects students to share out loud some of their transitions.

(Continued)

(Continued)

Peer Revision
You need to be sure to model what good comments sound like during a peer session. Students can work with a partner on their revisions, or you can separate the class into groups based on their revision needs. You can create a class chart of what to look for as a reviewer. You might also choose to provide a guide for peer revision and editing. You can create them to focus on specific mini-lessons (see sample Resource N: Peer Revision Sheet for Expository Writing).

Editing Biographies
Based on the syntactic errors you see your students making as they draft their biographies, you will determine your mini-lessons on editing. Some editing lessons I have used when teaching biographies to my students have included: • **Verb tense.** The teacher will use her modeled writing piece to highlight her verbs. She will begin with the beginning of the biography, noting the use of past-tense verbs. Students can check their verb tenses in their own biographies. The teacher can continue this process by noting verb tenses in the middle and end of her biography. • **Capitalization rules (proper nouns).** Teachers will provide explicit instruction on capitalizing proper nouns, including the name of their biography subject, date of birth, birthplace, including city, state, country, and other noted proper nouns included in students' biographies. • **Punctuating dates.** Since dates, including date of birth, dates of key accomplishments, and date of death may be present in many biographies, an explicit lesson on punctuating dates is helpful.

Expanding our Biographies
Give students time to just work toward a final draft. They will continue to incorporate all of the previous mini-lessons, talk with their friends to improve their writing, and make final decisions before making their writing public. This can also include adding illustrations or pictures.

The Work of a Writer Is Never Done
When you think you are finished with your draft, go back to your list of possible subjects or other drafts you have started and continue to practice writing biographies. This helps give other students time to finish their writing while making sure that everyone is working purposefully to develop themselves as writers. Based on your individual work with students they may all be working on different ways to improve as writers of biographies.

Publishing
If you have time, the students can take their finished drafts and make a picture book of their biography. Otherwise you want to allow them time to make their writing presentable for an author's celebration. Be sure to invite all of the people the students wrote about.

Mrs. Angelica Machado's third grade class. Her class consists of Spanish-speaking ELs ranging from preproduction to "native-like fluency" levels of second language acquisition. The structure and components of the instructional sequence are similar to those presented in Chapter 2 for writing a personal narrative. You will continue to see examples of what teachers might say to introduce the lessons, followed by a focused objective for the mini-lesson, independent practice, and a share component.

Many parts of the instructional writing sequence presented were developed with particular attention to the needs of ELs. Specifically, some elements of the instructional sequence that provided language and literacy scaffolds for ELs included:

- Students were given the opportunity to read and retell biographies at the inception of the lesson sequence. The exposure and practice in orally retelling a biography begins the process of developing the language of biographies.
- With a partner, students researched how biographies are written using an age-appropriate and reader-appropriate text.
- Students were allowed to talk about their work as writers EVERY lesson based on the mini-lesson of the day.
- The teacher provided think-alouds and modeled writing every step of the way, making written English visible for students.
- Breaking up the draft in sections, beginning, middle, and end, with attention to the generalizations of biographies, provides the scaffolding ELs need to understand how to write a biography in English.

The instructional sequence above can be used to teach biography the first time the students are exposed to it in their perspective grade level. However, as they begin to develop a familiarity with the genre of biography, the teacher will not need to provide as many scaffolds along the way. You want to gradually release the responsibility to the students to engage in their own process as they prepare and create a draft of a biography. In addition, depending on your students' needs, you may chose to leave lessons out, add additional lessons, or take more time with any one writing objective. The lesson sequence is to give teachers an idea of how you can carefully scaffold an expository genre for ELs. I also like to provide students with a rubric that highlights what we have learned as writers of exposition. Figure 3.8, Biography Rubric, is a sample I have used for evaluating my students' biographies. You can always tailor your rubrics to account for the specific lessons you have covered during your writing unit.

Figure 3.9, "Angelica Lopez Real," and Figure 3.10, "Biography," are samples from two students in Mrs. Machado's class who completed their drafts based on the instructional writing sequence. Figure 3.9 was written by Evelyn, who at the time was at a "speech emergent stage" in her second language acquisition. Sara, who wrote Figure 3.10, is an English-only student. In both cases you can see that the discourse structure of the biography is in place. This was a result of the scaffolding of the draft and the emphasis on elements of biography. From this point on the teacher can help them revise and edit accordingly.

In Evelyn's piece you will notice that she will need additional help on how to delete insignificant information and add more details to the key moments and events in her subject's life. However, for a student in the early stages of second language acquisition, you can tell that Evelyn felt a sense of comfort in writing her draft. She uses her own voice and wants to share everything she learned about her subject. Now that she feels successful in the completion of a

4	THE SUBJECT IS CLEARLY IDENTIFIED IN THE INTRODUCTION
	BIOGRAPHY FOLLOWS A LOGICAL CHRONOLOGY OF THE PERSON'S LIFE
	INFORMATION IS GROUPED TOGETHER TO MAINTAIN A FOCUS
	EACH PARAGRAPH HAS A MAIN IDEA WITH MANY SUPPORTING DETAILS AND INFORMATION
	PROPER VERB TENSE IS USED THROUGHOUT TO THE ESSAY
	LITTLE TO NO SPELLING ERRORS
3	THE SUBJECT IS IDENTIFIED
	BIOGRAPHY FOLLOWS A LOGICAL CHRONOLOGY OF THE PERSON'S LIFE WITH SOME INFORMATION OUT OF PLACE
	INFORMATION IS GROUPED TOGETHER TO MAINTAIN A FOCUS
	EACH PARAGRAPH HAS A MAIN IDEA WITH SOME SUPPORTING DETAILS AND INFORMATION
	PROPER VERB TENSE IS USED, WITH SOME ERRORS
	SOME SPELLING ERRORS BUT DO NOT DISTRACT FROM THE CONTENT
2	THE SUBJECT IS IDENTIFIED AT SOME POINT IN THE BIOGRAPHY
	BIOGRAPHY INCLUDES DIFFERENT TIMES IN THE PERSON'S LIFE, BUT NOT NECESSARILY IN ORDER
	INFORMATION IS DISJOINTED, OFTEN SHIFTING OFF TOPIC FROM ONE PARAGRAPH TO THE NEXT
	EACH PARAGRAPH HAS A MAIN IDEA BUT WITH LITTLE SUPPORT OR INFORMATION
	THERE ARE ERRORS IN VERB TENSE BUT THIS DOES NOT DISTRACT FROM THE CONTENT
	SPELLING ERRORS ARE PRESENT BUT DO NOT DISTRACT FROM THE CONTENT
1	THE SUBJECT IS NOT IDENTIFIED IN THE BIOGRAPHY
	BIOGRAPHY SKIPS AROUND AND PRESENTS FRAGMENTS OF THE PERSON'S LIFE WITH NO ORGANIZATION
	INFORMATION IS WRITTEN RANDOMLY
	PARAGRAPHS DO NOT HAVE A MAIN IDEA WITH LITTLE TO NO SUPPORTING DETAILS AND INFORMATION
	CONTAINS IMPROPER VERB TENSE THROUGHOUT THE ESSAY
	MANY SPELLING ERRORS THAT DISTRACT FROM THE CONTENT OF THE ESSAY

Figure 3.8 Biography Rubric

draft, we can be very purposeful on what we will choose to focus on as we develop her written language.

In Sara's draft you will see that she has already begun to make self-editing and revision marks throughout her draft. On page three she writes a note to herself to get more information from her dad that was missing. She writes and circles the words, "ask dad" a few times to indicate the location in her text where the missing information is needed.

In both cases the girls are working at their own pace and developmental level as a writer in English. All the while they are both learning how to write a biography. As they continue to develop their English and continue to read biographies, they will improve their writing.

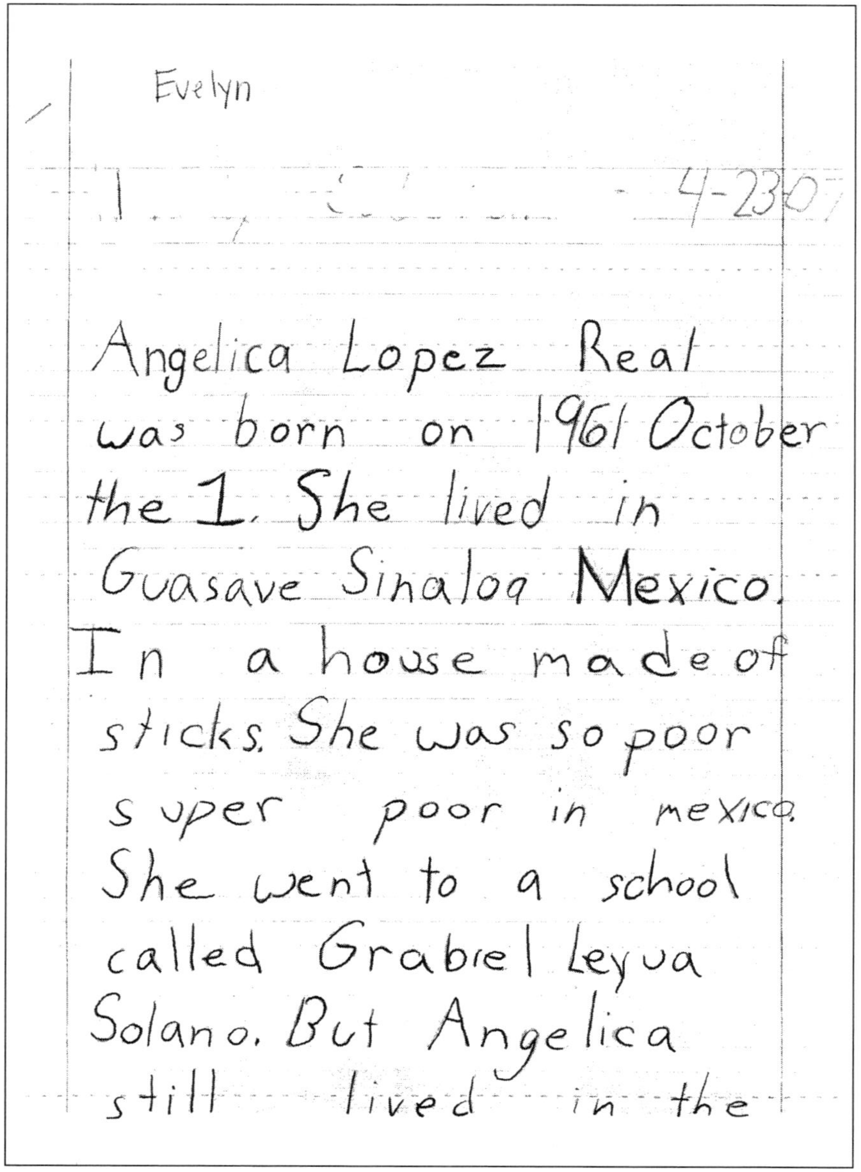

Evelyn

4-230

Angelica Lopez Real
was born on 1961 October
the 1. She lived in
Guasave Sinaloa Mexico.
In a house made of
sticks. She was so poor
super poor in mexico.
She went to a school
called Grabrel leyva
Solano. But Angelica
still lived in the

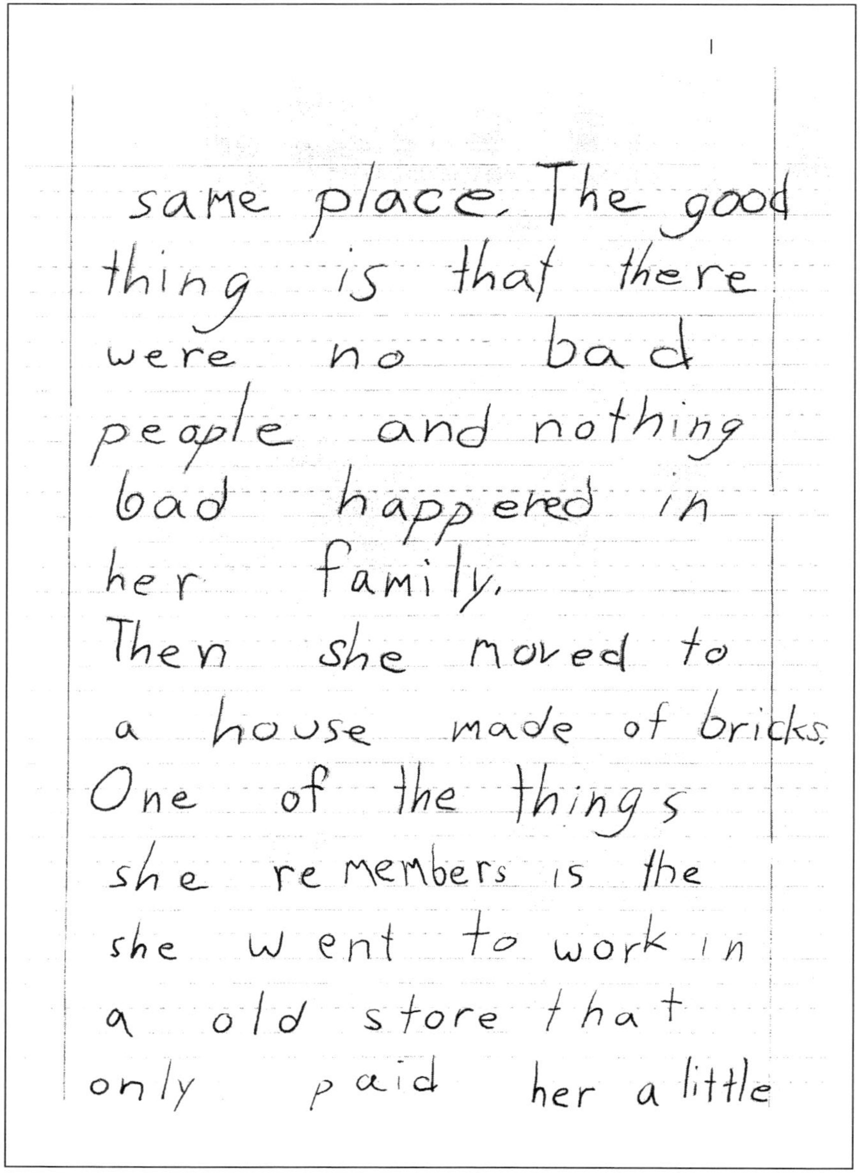

same place. The good
thing is that there
were no bad
people and nothing
bad happered in
her family.
Then she moved to
a house made of bricks.
One of the things
she remembers is the
she went to work in
a old store that
only paid her a little

Figure 3.9 "Angelica Lopez Real"

(Continued)

lives in a blue house. And I forgot to tell you that she works in our house taking care of a baby called Nicky and she goes to school to lern inglish. She remembers that she liked her life alot. See you later.

bit of money. She look up to her uncle and her grandmother. It was hard to take care of my sister. She liked to be known for her hole life. One thing she likes the best in the goverment that there were no slaves. Write how she

(Continued)

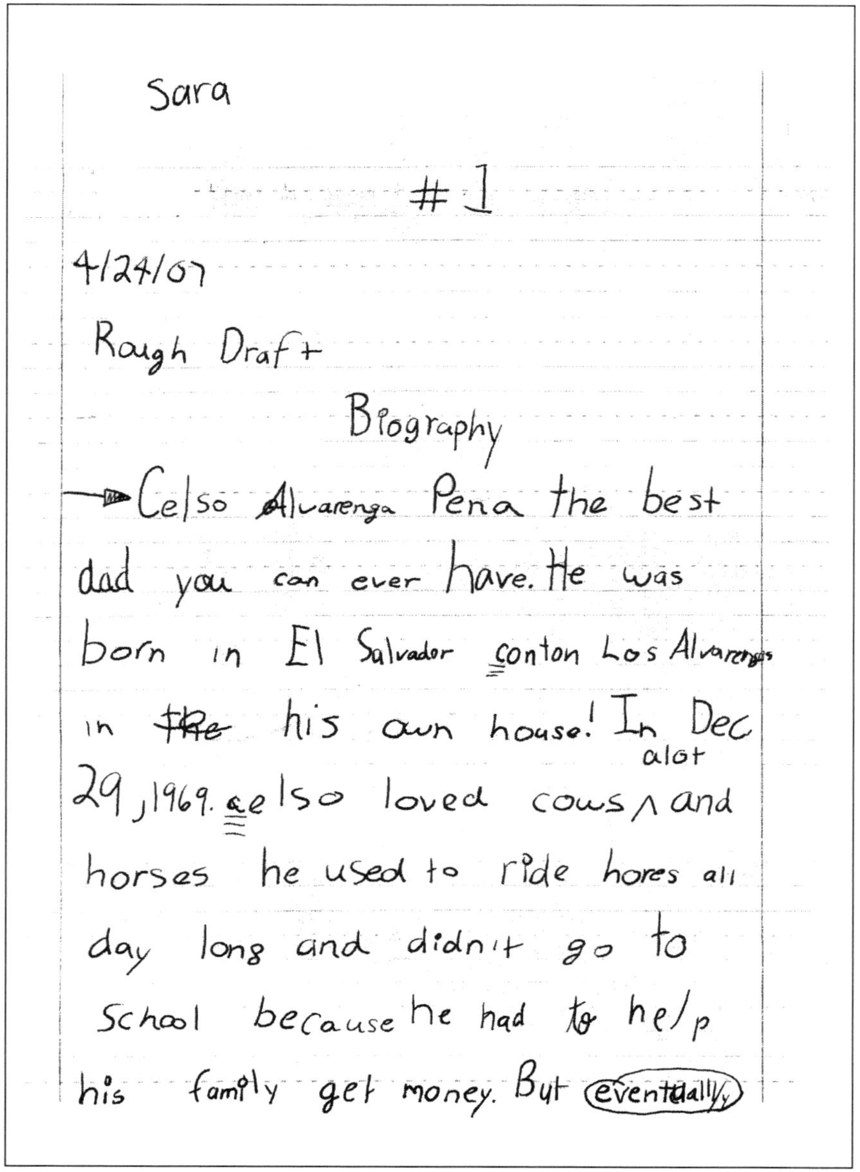

Sara

#1

4/24/07

Rough Draft

Biography

→ Celso Alvarenga Pena the best dad you can ever have. He was born in El Salvador Conton Los Alvarenga in the his own house! In Dec 29, 1969. Celso loved cows and horses he used to ride hores all day long and didn't go to School because he had to help his family get money. But eventually

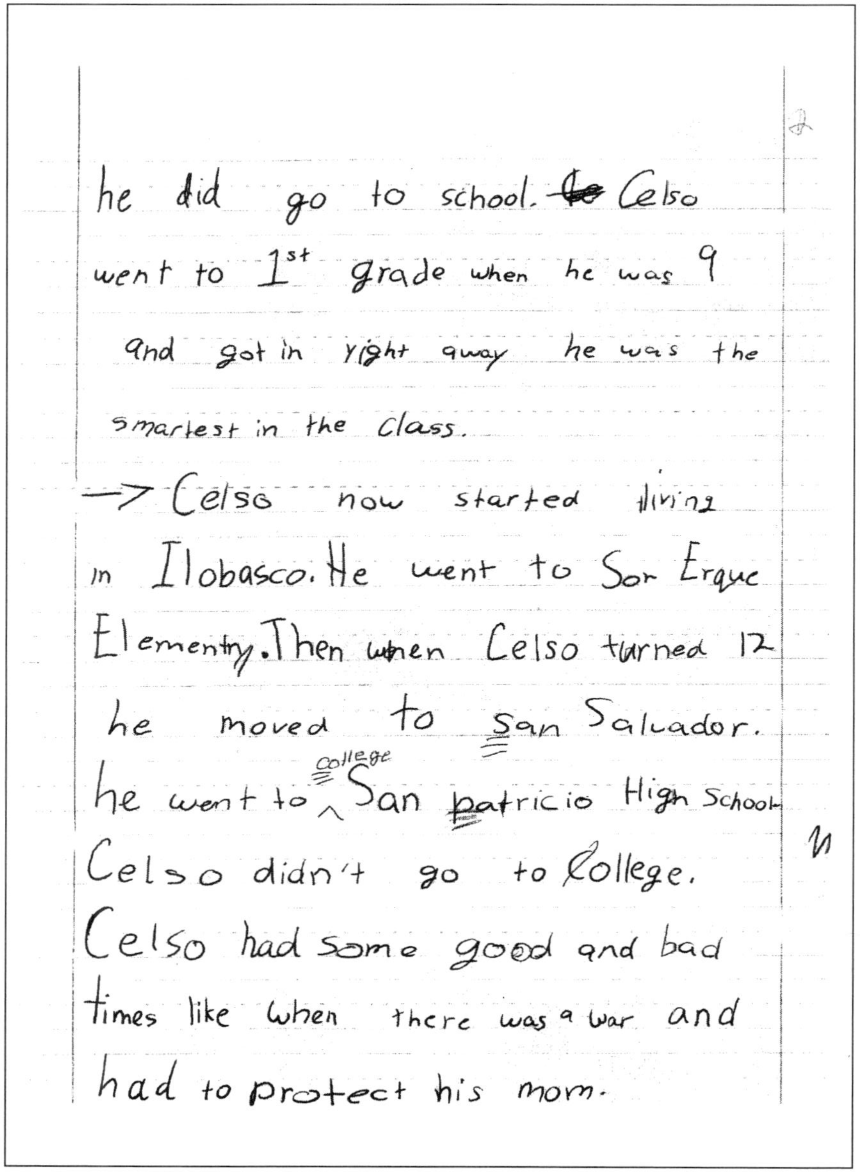

he did go to school. Celso went to 1st grade when he was 9 and got in right away he was the smartest in the Class.

→ Celso now started living in Ilobasco. He went to Sor Erque Elementry. Then when Celso turned 12 he moved to San Salvador. he went to San Patricio High School Celso didn't go to College. Celso had some good and bad times like when there was a war and had to protect his mom.

Figure 3.10 "Biography"

(Continued)

He He was always was with his mom

because they got (devorced), but

he still sees his dad. He looked

up to mom, dad, and his nice friend.

→ When Celso was A he became

a man he told his mom that

he was going to the united States to

have a better life and he went walking.

and

Sailed. Celso got here at the age

of (his dad). Then he made a

friend. named (his dad). Celso needed

money so (the friend) told him there

---

was a job at Taco bell and

he said then. He went and

met my ₁Magda and they fell in
        mom

love. Now Celso is an area coach

and does lots of work every days.

he maried Magda they had two

Children named Rebecca and Alexandra.
                                    have two
They drive @ houses one in LA and

one in El Salvador. He says that

he wants to known for the

kind and respectful man. Celso lives

in Los Angales. Hes still an area

coach manages 6 stores & gms.

Celso loves to play soccer, basket

ball and collects watches for fun, and

old dollar bills.

MAKING IT PUBLIC

The benefit about publishing exposition is that it envelopes us in our daily lives. "Writing should not be viewed as an activity that happens only within a class-room's walls. Teachers need to support students in the development of writing lives, habits, and preferences for life outside school …. As much as possible, instruction should be geared toward making sense in a life outside of school, so that writing has ample room to grow in individuals' lives" (Writing Study Group of the National Council of Teachers of English [NCTE], 2004). We see examples of nonfiction in newspapers and magazines, and on television, radio, and the Internet. We need to provide opportunities for our students to publish nonfiction in authentic ways that connect to students' outside world. Most nonfiction writing is published in a traditional essay. Though it is important for our students to learn how to write in traditional forms, if we really want to get their attention and develop writers, we need to think outside the box. Figure 3.11, Publishing Exposition, shares some ideas for publishing exposition in more interesting and worldly ways. What I usually suggest to my teachers is to allow students to follow the writing process and prepare a traditional draft of the essay, but when it comes to publishing their draft, let them publish in some of the ways shared in the figure. This way they learn how to write the traditional essay they will be responsible for on their writing assessments, while the final writing product is more inviting and enjoyable.

CONCLUSION

The key to writing exposition with students is the development of background knowledge through ample time for researching. We gather information for expository writing from the world around us. Unlike narrative writing, exposition stretches beyond one's own imagination. You begin with what you know on a subject and work toward expanding your knowledge base. Students need choice in what they will research to acknowledge their curiosities and passion and ultimately motivate them to want to write. In addition, taking time to publish their research in more creative ways can further engage reluctant writers. Students need to be guided on *how* to research and *where* they can access information to create richer expository text. Without the knowledge base on a topic, what students are able to do as writers is limited. Expository writing is factual. So they need the opportunity to find the facts and the guidance to present them effectively.

Expository Genre	Ways to Go Public
Biography	Write a script for a movie about the person
Autobiography	Perform an episode for the Biography channel
	Scrapbook
	Obituaries
	Museum exhibit brochure
	Documentaries
Process Writing	Board game directions
	Class recipe book
	How-to publication for Home Depot
	Self-improvement book
Reports	Newscast (Resource O: Preparing a newscast)
	Feature article
	Commentaries
	Meet the press
	Talk show (expert guests)
	Panel discussion
	Political cartoons/cartoon strips
	Speech at a conference on your topic (can make a PowerPoint presentation as well)
Description	Documentaries
	School/community newsletter
	Museum, zoo, farm . . . brochures
	Catalogues
	Informational picture books for a younger audience
	Travel guides
	Business letter (complaint letter)
	Posters/billboards
Response to Literature	Book review for BarnesandNoble.com
	Book review in a magazine or newspaper
	Book cover (inside cover, back cover)

Figure 3.11   Publishing Exposition

RESOURCES FOR TEACHING EXPOSITORY WRITING

Crafting Expository Argument: Practical Approaches to the Writing Process for Students and Teachers, Michael Degen

Expository Writing, Emily Hutchinson

Improving the Expository Writing Skills of Adolescents, Robert J. Kanellas, Lorraine Dagostino, and Carifio James

Investigate Nonfiction: The Reading/Writing Teacher's Companion, Donald Graves

Is That a Fact?: Teaching Nonfiction Writing K-3, Tony Stead

Listen to This: Developing an Ear for Expository, Marcia S. Freeman

Literature Models to Teach Expository Writing K-5, Susan Anderson-McElveen, Connie Campbell Dierking

Nonfiction Craft Lessons: Teaching Writing K-8, Ralph Fletcher, JoAnn Portalupi

Nonfiction Matters: Reading, Writing, and Research 3-8, Stephanie Harvey

The Norton Reader: An Anthology of Expository Prose, Linda H. Peterson, John C. Brereton (editors)

Persuasive Writing 4

Photo by Eugenia Mora-Flores.

*W*hat if the freedom of choice was taken from you? Everyday in the United States we have the chance to make choices about everything we do. There are laws and rules we follow to keep each other safe, but we still have the right to make choices. So why do adults always find ways to take choices away from kids. My school recently asked the parents to vote on whether or not we should wear school uniforms. They are taking away our freedom to choose what we want to wear. I am strongly against school uniforms at our school. I realize parents and teachers would argue that uniforms help kids focus on school better, that it keeps kids from teasing each other about their clothes, and that it is cheaper to have uniforms. But I don't think school uniforms really make that much of a difference on how kids behave or do in school.

What kids wear to school doesn't really effect how they pay attention and participate in school. Teachers think that clothes are a distraction and that if we take away free dress kids won't be distracted by cool clothes or shoes. This is just an excuse. Kids *don't pay attention in class for other reasons besides clothes and shoes. They like to talk about things they did on the weekends or they like to draw and play with other things like pencils and pens. Even if kids had to wear uniforms they would still be distracted. The teacher has to get tough if kids don't behave and have fun activities to keep kids excited about school.*

Kids always tease one another. Even if kids wore uniforms they would still find something mean to say to each other. Teachers think that if we wore school uniforms kids wouldn't tease each other for not having the coolest shoes or for having old clothes. But the thing is that kids are just mean. They will tease about their hair, when they mess up at sports, when they fall down, or for how they talk. So school uniforms will not stop the teasing it will only make kids more angry because they had to wear the uniform and so they might even be meaner to their friends.

Parents think that it would be cheaper to buy uniforms than regular clothes. They might be right but what if the uniforms are expensive. Some uniforms cost more than regular pants or shorts or shirts. I would argue that if anything the price would be the same. Plus, can you imagine how many uniforms my mom or dad would have to buy so that they won't have to wash my clothes every day. It will cost more having to wash the uniforms all the time. Plus the regular clothes that we wear are already paid for because we have to change into something when we get home. We don't wear uniforms on the weekends or after school. So actually our parents would have to spend extra to buy uniforms because it is not the clothes we already have and wear.

Students should not have to wear uniforms, it takes away from their freedom of choice and there are no strong arguments that say we should. It doesn't help kids pay attention more, it doesn't stop teasing, and it might even cost more to wear them. If teachers have better activities to keep kids interested at school and administrators get stricter about teasing then there are really no reasons why uniforms would be better than free dress!

—Elias, 2003

UNDERSTANDING PERSUASIVE WRITING

Unknowingly, students spend their days and nights preparing for persuasive writing. Day in and day out they are working tirelessly to convince their parents, their friends, and their teachers of many things. In addition, students are bombarded with examples of persuasive writing through the media. At every turn there is an advertisement, a commercial, a billboard trying to persuade them to buy the latest electronic game console or cell phone. When teaching persuasive writing we need to tap into these experiences to help students understand the purpose of persuasion—to try and get people to agree with you. It is how we manipulate and convince others to believe what we say, do as we ask, and act in our favor.

Persuasive writing (rhetoric) may seem to be a very opinionative type of writing, but it is grounded in facts and a strong voice to back up one's opinion. Persuasive writing is intended to convince the reader that a certain point of view is the right one. It utilizes logic and reason to show that one idea is more legitimate than another. Persuasive writing can be characterized by the following:

- Presentation of an argument, a clear stance
- Clearly explains the issue or position
- Arguments for both sides are presented
- Compelling evidence, sound reasoning, details, facts, logical reasoning, quotations from experts, or examples are presented to support the writer's stance

The ability to get into the head, the thoughts and the feelings of someone else to determine how to persuade them is challenging. For this reason we often do not see persuasive writing as a standard until fifth grade. In order to present a convincing argument you have to understand your topic from multiple perspectives. Jean Piaget (1983) in his theory of *cognitive development* believed that a child is able to accomplish this in the *formal operations* stage. At this stage, typically beginning around age eleven, children are able to think abstractly and understand multiple perspectives. The ability to understand someone else's thoughts, feelings, and perspectives becomes possible. The best arguments are those that address the perspective of the intended audience.

Think about when you hear a young child try and convince their parents to let them play outside a little longer. Their reasons typically consist of, "Because I want to," "It's fun," or "Why not?" Young children are not yet able to see why it is that their parents do not want them to go outside, while older students are equipped with the knowledge base to counter their parents' ideas. Let's think about this same scenario with an older child. His responses may include, "If you give me more time, it will give you a chance to finish up what it is you need to do so I won't get in your way," or "In giving me more time outside I will be more active and stay fit, but if I come in I would probably just be sitting down either watching TV or playing my PlayStation, and it could lead to childhood obesity. Do you want to be the cause of that?" These types of arguments begin to play with parents' minds, in some ways turning the argument against them, making them feel guilty for not abiding. Adolescents are VERY intelligent, very creative thinkers. We need to hone in on these skills and make them fabulous persuasive writers.

PERSUASIVE ESSAYS

To provide the foundations for persuasive writing, English learners (ELs) need to learn a basic discourse structure for preparing and defending an argument or position. Figure 4.1, Persuasive Essay Discourse Structure, provides an overview of the key components included in a persuasive essay.

Introduction	Body	Conclusion
Thesis: Argument, position, stance, or point of view presented. Introduce your three key arguments or reasons to support thesis.	Each argument/reason presented in the introduction will be separated out by paragraphs. Minimum of three paragraphs. Opposing viewpoint(s) are presented.	Restate argument or position (thesis). Summarize main points. Personal statement/call to action.

Figure 4.1 Persuasive Essay Discourse Structure

The difficulty of writing a persuasive essay is in the preparation of the argument. Thinking about the counterarguments and the rebuttal from the opposition is challenging. To help students prepare for persuasive writing they need varied opportunities to talk. Students need to collect multiple perspectives and opinions to strengthen their argument. They need to elicit counterarguments to prepare a defense in support of their position. Once the students have brainstormed ideas, reasons, and counterarguments, they need guidance for organizing their ideas. Organizing persuasive writing into a written essay should be carefully scaffolded for ELs.

In Figure 4.2, I provide an example of a comprehensive instructional writing sequence for scaffolding persuasive writing. This sequence has been used with ELs in fifth through eighth grades to prepare them for a persuasive essay. The samples provided throughout the sequence came from my work with a fifth grade class of Spanish-speaking ELs. Each lesson includes an introduction, a focused mini-lesson, opportunities for independent practice, and talk (share). The main objective of each lesson is highlighted in the mini-lesson.

The instructional writing sequence presented (beginning on page 73) was developed with particular attention to the needs of ELs. However, depending on your class and their unique writing needs, the lessons may need adaptations or modifications. In addition, the length of time needed to develop students' persuasive essays will also vary. When I implemented the writing sequence, each lesson took one day. However, it is likely that in many cases students would need additional time and support at any stage of the process. The lesson sequence is simply an example of how to carefully scaffold persuasive writing for ELs. Specifically, some elements of the instructional sequence that provided language and literacy scaffolds for ELs included:

- Prewriting! There is a great deal of time spent on the development of ideas using a variety of graphic organizers and talking with classmates. All of the preparation for writing helps ELs determine the language they will want to use when writing their essay.
- Graphic organizers. The use of a variety of graphic organizers helps ELs organize their ideas using short bits of written language. They do not have to write out complete thoughts at this point. They can jot down words, phrases, or, if ready, full sentences as they prepare to draft. Once all of their ideas have been organized into the final "persuasive essay" graphic organizer, they can focus on their written English to flesh out their thinking in writing.
- Talk, talk, talk! Most of the lessons provide opportunities for students to check their thinking and writing with a partner. They share ideas, and provide oral and written language support. Working with a partner in a comfortable setting lowers the affective filter (Krashen, 1981), facilitating learning. English learners feel safe talking with a partner around their writing. It is a less intimidating setting for trying out oral and written language.

(Text continued on p. 80)

What Is Persuasive Writing?

Introduction: Oral brainstorm with the class, "What does it mean to persuade someone?" Record students' responses. Explain to the students that they will be beginning a unit of study on persuasive writing and that to persuade someone of something takes a great deal of planning and preparation.

Mini-lesson: **Understanding persuasive writing.** Read *Earrings!* by Judith Viorst. This is a short picture book that does a nice job of presenting the key elements for a persuasive argument.

After reading the story ask the students the following:

- What did the girl in the book want? (her argument)
- Who was she trying to persuade? (audience)
- What were some of her main arguments for why she should get her ears pierced? (reasons)
- Why did her parents say she couldn't get earrings for pierced ears? (counterarguments)

Record their responses to the questions above. Once they have been recorded, label them by their role in persuasive writing. See parentheses following each question above. Explain to students that these are the elements of persuasive writing. The teacher will then focus the students on the "audience," who they will try to persuade. She will model a list of possible "audiences" to address for persuasive writing. For example: her friends, children, husband, mother, father, sister, boss, colleagues, and professors.

Independent writing time: Invite students to think about all of the different people they have tried to persuade of something. Have the students generate a list of possible audiences for persuasive writing (for example, their parents, friends, teachers . . .). This will only take about 10 minutes.

Share: Students will share their list with a partner and add additional ideas to their list after sharing.

Developing Arguments

Introduction: The teacher will remind students of the elements of persuasive writing from the day before. Explain that today they will begin to think about what it is they want to write about.

Mini-lesson: **Generating possible topics.** "Looking back at some of the people you put on your list yesterday, we will today be thinking about the many things we try to convince them of. For example, let's start with the principal. What are the things you would try to convince or persuade your principal to do?" Record the students' responses in a basic web (see below). This will begin to generate a list of possible topics to write about.

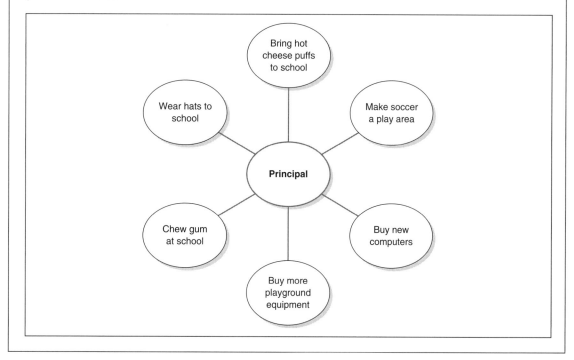

Figure 4.2 Instructional Writing Sequence for Writing a Persuasive Essay   *(Continued)*

(Continued)

Independent writing: Students will use their list of possible audiences they created the day before and begin to brainstorm for each person different things of which they might try to convince them. The goal is for each student to have created at least one web, but many students will have multiple webs depending on how quickly they work.

Share: Have students share their webs with a partner and elicit additional suggestions for possible arguments.

Introduction: "To write a persuasive essay you want to be knowledgeable about your position. Today we are going to think about which argument we can best develop."

Mini-lesson: **Selecting a topic.** Using the web from the day before, model a think-aloud for selecting a topic. "Looking at the web of possible arguments for the principal, I am thinking about which ones I think I know enough about to try and convince her to side with my position." The teacher will continue to think aloud about each one, starring the one's she thinks may be a good choice. "I think new computers would be a great idea as well as making soccer a play area. I should think about which one I know a lot about and could argue best. So, since I am such a huge soccer fan and I know what it would take to make soccer a play area, I think I will pick that one."

Independent writing: Students will review their webs and begin to narrow down their topic choice.

Share: The teacher will call on a few students to share out loud the topic they decided on and why.

Determining Reasons to Argue

Introduction: "Now that we have selected our topic, we want to think about all the reasons why anyone should believe us and want to side with our argument."

Mini-lesson: **Developing an argument.** The teacher will use a graphic organizer to develop her argument (see Resource P: Preparing My Position). The teacher can elicit ideas from the students to complete her organizer. You can also use a simple bubble map to brainstorm opinions/reasons.

ARGUMENT	OPINIONS/REASONS
SOCCER SHOULD BE A PLAY AREA	STUDENTS LOVE SOCCER
	EQUIPMENT IS CHEAP
	MORE STUDENTS CAN GET INVOLVED

Independent writing: The students will begin to fill out their organizer. If they finish early they can begin a new organizer for a different argument.

Share: Have students share their reasons with a classmate and elicit more ideas.

Debating

Introduction: "We sometimes think we have all the right reasons, but unless we can try them out on someone, we might be surprised. Today you will get a chance to debate your argument, or position, with your classmates."

Mini-lesson: **Addressing the audience: counterarguments.** The teacher should invite two students to model a mini-debate. The teacher will begin by telling the two students that she thinks the school should have a designated soccer area at recess and lunch. She shares all of her reasons why, and the students then get a chance to counter her reasons. They can address any of her reasons, posing counterarguments and reasons of their own why soccer should NOT be a designated play area. The teacher will then jot down notes on the "Addressing the Audience" graphic organizer, Resource Q. At this point only the first two columns of the organizer will be completed. The reason(s) column comes directly from their brainstorm of the lesson before, on preparing their position.

REASON(S)	COUNTERARGUMENTS	EVIDENCE
EVERYONE LOVES SOCCER	MANY STUDENTS DON'T PLAY SOCCER. THEY PREFER TO PLAY BASEBALL AND OTHER SPORTS.	
EQUIPMENT IS CHEAP	THERE IS NO MONEY FOR NEW EQUIPMENT. NEED GOAL POSTS AND NEW SOCCER BALLS.	
MORE STUDENTS CAN GET INVOLVED	STUDENTS CAN GET HURT WITH SO MANY BODIES PLAYING TOGETHER.	

Independent writing/share: The students will be divided up into triads. Each student will get a chance to debate his position/argument to his classmates. After each student has shared his position to his classmates, he should take about two to three minutes to jot down any notes, new reasons, and counterarguments shared by peers.

Supporting Your Argument

Introduction: The teacher will remind students that they had a chance to hear from their "mock" audience the day before. "Today you will have a chance to work on how you will defend or support your position. You must provide specific and convincing evidence, not broad generalizations or personal opinions. You need to research both sides of the issue to provide a stronger argument."

Mini-lesson: **Supporting an argument with evidence.** Returning to the graphic organizer from the day before, "Addressing Your Audience," the teacher will share how you can support your argument, through facts, quotes, statistics, and examples. Figure 4.3, Ways to Support an Argument, located after the instructional writing sequence, provides examples of various types of support you can share with your students. The teacher will return to her graphic organizer from the day before and model how to fill out the third column.

REASON(S)	COUNTERARGUMENTS	EVIDENCE
EVERYONE LOVES SOCCER	MANY STUDENTS DON'T PLAY SOCCER. THEY PREFER TO PLAY BASEBALL AND OTHER SPORTS.	NEARLY 3 MILLION CHILDREN AGES FIVE TO NINETEEN PLAY SOCCER.
EQUIPMENT IS CHEAP	THERE IS NO MONEY FOR NEW EQUIPMENT. NEED GOAL POSTS AND NEW SOCCER BALLS.	FAMILIES CAN DONATE SOCCER BALLS AND SCHOOL CONES CAN BE USED AS GOAL POSTS.
MORE STUDENTS CAN GET INVOLVED	STUDENTS CAN GET HURT WITH SO MANY BODIES PLAYING TOGETHER.	PROPER YARD SUPERVISION CAN PROHIBIT INJURIES.

Independent writing: Students will complete their "Addressing Your Audience" organizer by filling out the third column to address the counterarguments.

Share: They will share their evidence with a classmate and elicit additional supports for their argument (an optional organizer you can use to develop students' arguments is presented in Resource R: Defending Your Argument).

Preparing Your Position Statement

Introduction: "Now that you have thought out your argument in response to possible counterarguments from your audience, we are ready to craft our position statements (thesis)."

(Continued)

(Continued)

Mini-lesson: **Writing a thesis.** The teacher will model the development of her position statement, also referred to as the thesis. The thesis will include her three strongest reasons for her argument. For example, "Soccer should be a play area available at recess and lunch because it is a popular sport, equipment is easily accessible, and it will get more students involved."

Independent writing: The students will draft a possible position statement (thesis).

Share: Have the students share their thesis statements for feedback.

Planning for Writing

Introduction: "We have taken our time preparing our arguments and gathering all of the information and ideas we will need to plan out our essays."

Mini-lesson: **Organizing ideas for writing.** The teacher will use her organizer, addressing the audience, and her thesis statement to begin to plan out her essay. Using Resource S: Planning for Persuasive Writing the teacher will model her plan.

Independent writing: The students will fill out their "Planning for Persuasive Writing" organizer.

Share: The teacher will select one or two students to present their organizer for class feedback.

The Introduction

Introduction: "We are ready to write. Today we will begin to write our persuasive essays."

Mini-lesson: **Drafting the introduction.** The teacher will share the article, "Hooked." This article was taken from *Write Time for Kids, Level 3*. You can use any piece of persuasive text that can serve as a model for writing an introduction. After reading the article ask the students to look closely at the introduction. "What do you notice the author includes in the introduction?" The students typically notice the position statement, the reasons/arguments, and the audience is presented. As the students identify different components of the introduction, label them on the text. She will make the connection for the students that what they noticed matches the first portion of their graphic organizer, "Planning for Persuasive Writing." The teacher will then model her introduction. For example:

GOOOOOAAAALLLLLLL!!!!!!! What a wonderful sound to hear. The world has been taken over by soccer. Everywhere you go, every park you pass you see kids kicking around a soccer ball, taking shots on goal. Nearly 3 million children ages five to nineteen play soccer all over the world. It is a wonder why our school does not include soccer as one of its play areas. The principal might argue that soccer is a dangerous sport and we don't have enough room on our field for soccer. I would argue soccer should be a play area available at recess and lunch because it is a popular sport, equipment is easily accessible and it will get more students involved.

Independent writing: Students will draft their introductions using their planning organizer.

Share: One or two students will be asked to read aloud their introduction for class feedback.

A Strong Opening

Introduction: "When writing a persuasive essay you want to be sure to capture your audiences' attention if you really want to convince them, or persuade them to your side."

Mini-lesson: **A strong opening.** The teacher will display a sample persuasive text from a commentary by Leonard Pitts Jr. (2000) from *The Miami Herald*. She will ask the students, "What do you notice about how he began his commentary?"

"HERE'S something to make your day . . . miserable.

"The National Center for Education Statistics, a branch of the U.S. Department of Education, reports that in 1998, 38 percent of the nation's fourth-graders were below basic, the lowest level of reading ability. Nearly a quarter of high school seniors were similarly unable to perform.

"So it's easy to understand why concerned parents would march down to the library and demand that something be done about witches . . ." ("Illiteracy Is What Really Scares Me," 2000).

The students will share that they notice he starts with a "hook" followed by a "statistic" and an "action." The teacher should record these ideas on large chart paper entitled, "Great Openings" or "How to Write Strong Openings."

Independent practice: The teacher will distribute various persuasive texts for students to review. I like using *Write Time for Kids* and Leonard Pitt's commentaries because they provide a lot of variety and creativity. With a partner they will read their assigned text and determine what type of information the author is using in the opening.

Share: Each partnership will share what they found and the teacher should record new ideas to the class chart on strong openings.

Introduction: Remind students that the day before they identified various ways to start a persuasive essay. Point out the examples on the class chart. "Today we will look at our own openings to our essays and revise them to make them great openings."

Mini-lesson: **Developing a strong opening.** There are various ways of introducing an argument. "We want to make sure we start off with a bang so we get our audience to listen." The teacher will select three different types of openings from the list the class generated the day before and craft three possible openings for her argument. For example it can begin with one of the following:

- Opening with an unusual detail
- Opening with a strong statement
- Opening with a quotation
- Opening with an anecdote
- Opening with a statistic or fact
- Opening with a question
- Opening with an exaggeration or outrageous statement

Independent writing: The students will prepare three different types of openings for their position/argument.

Share: Have students share their three openings for feedback. They will revise their opening based on their partner's feedback.

Moving the Draft Forward

Introduction: "Now that we have improved our introduction we can move forward with our essay."

Mini-lesson: **Drafting the body of the essay.** Going back to her persuasive writing plan, the teacher will focus on paragraph #2 and continue her draft.

Independent writing: The students will draft paragraph #2 using their persuasive writing plan to focus their writing.

Share: The teacher will select one or two students to read out loud their second paragraph for class feedback.

Drafting paragraphs #3 and #4 will follow the same lesson format used for paragraph #2. Students should see the teacher model each paragraph using her "Planning for Persuasive Writing" graphic organizer to keep each paragraph focused on one reason at a time. Students will continue to move their draft forward.

(Continued)

(Continued)

Revision

Based on what you notice about your students' drafts, you will make decisions on the types of revision lessons they will need. Some revision lessons I have done with students include:

- **Transition words** (See Resource T: Persuasive Writing Transition Words): After modeling how to include them in my writing, the students are each given the list, cut Resource T vertically, to add transition words to their drafts.
- **Embellish your argument**: The students are shown how to add information to each paragraph to embellish their argument. This includes rewriting sentences to make them more descriptive as well as adding more examples or information to make their point stronger. You can use Figure 4.3, Ways to Support an Argument, as a resource to develop individual mini-lessons to help students enhance their arguments.
- **Ways of arguing**: Students are shown additional ways to argue a point. They can revisit each supporting paragraph and determine if they want to make any changes to the way they argued their point. For example:

Arguing both sides: Within each supporting paragraph the students can present pros and cons to consider both sides of the argument. Or, they can add a fifth paragraph that presents the opposing point of view and reply with a rebuttal to the opposition. This makes the audience believe that the author is impartial and open-minded.

Arguing by analogy: Demonstrating that your argument is related to something else and can yield similar results gives strength to your argument. Keeping your audience in mind, make a comparison to something familiar and credible and show how it connects to your argument.

Arguing by authority: Begin your arguments with a credible source, testimonials, or eye witness accounts to enhance validity. You can speak as an expert yourself or use a recognizable authority that supports your position.

Peer Revision

Introduction: "Now that we have worked really hard on preparing our drafts up to this point, it's a good time to check how we are doing before we finish it."

Mini-lesson: **Peer revision**. The teacher will display a "Peer Revision" sheet (see Resource U: Peer Revision Sheet for Persuasive Writing). Explain to the students that it is always a good idea to check your work with a friend to see if your argument is well developed and supported. The teacher will pass out a copy of the "Peer Revision" sheet to each student. She will then display the persuasive text she has been creating all along. The teacher will then read her piece and ask her students to orally review her persuasive essay using the "Peer Revision" sheet provided. One question (from the "Peer Revision" sheet) at a time, the teacher will call on students to respond to her persuasive essay. They will not write on the "Peer Revision" sheet at this time; they have it to follow along. Continue until all parts of the sheet have been completed orally about the teacher's essay.

Share: The students will be partnered up to engage in a peer revision session. Each partner will use the "Peer Revision" sheet distributed to fill out based on his or her partner's essay. Once they have finished reading the essay and completing the "Peer Revision" sheet the students are to talk about their review.

Independent Writing: Students will now have a chance to revise their essay based on their partner's comments. The teacher should do the same based on the class feedback during the mini-lesson.

Conclusion

Introduction: "Now that you have had a chance to improve your essay, we are going to wrap up your argument with a concluding paragraph today."

Mini-lesson: **Writing the conclusion**. The teacher will take out her draft and model writing a conclusion using her "Persuasive Essay" organizer. She will think aloud what it is she is including in the conclusion.

For example, "So I will restate my argument one last time and remind my readers of my three strongest reasons why they should take my side. Then I have to end it with a powerful final statement."

Independent writing: The students will draft their conclusion using their "Persuasive Essay" organizer.

Share: The teacher will select one or two students to read their conclusions out loud for class feedback.

Finishing Strong

Introduction: "I have been thinking about how important it is to finish strong when writing a persuasive essay. You want your audience to feel like they have no other choice but to take your side. So let's think about how we can make our endings even stronger."

Mini-lesson: **Creating a strong finish**. The teacher will share that there are a variety of ways you can conclude an argument. For example:

With a question: Closing with a question lets your readers make their own predictions and draw their own conclusions.

With a recommendation: Closing with a recommendation provides your reader with examples of how they can move forward. It gives them a purpose.

With a quotation: Ending with a quote can provide a strong statement to synthesize your argument.

She will model two types of final statements for her concluding paragraph.

Independent writing/share: Students will create two types of final statements for their essay. They will share their two types of final statements with a partner for feedback and make a final decision on which to use.

Editing

You will want to determine editing lessons based on your students' needs. Some I have done in the past with students included separate mini-lessons on:

Complete and incomplete sentences

Possessive nouns

Regular and irregular past tense verbs

All of the above can be taught by modeling proper and improper grammar usage. I often record some improper sentences my students have used as the content for the lessons. I do not reference the student's name when using their samples. The students seem to understand the lessons better when they see sentences or excerpts from texts that are familiar and they could have written themselves. Once the grammar rules and generalizations are taught explicitly students should be asked to revisit their essays and focus their editing on the lesson of the day. After students have checked their own work they can double-check it with a peer.

Publishing

The students should be given time to prepare a final draft for publication. If possible, students should be allowed to use a word-processing program to type their final drafts. As early as fourth grade we see basic computer skills referenced in the California Language Arts Standards for writing. In addition to the traditional persuasive essay, Figure 4.5, Publishing Persuasive Text, at the end of the chapter provides alternatives for publishing persuasive writing.

- Scaffolding the draft. Every paragraph of the draft is discussed, modeled, and written one paragraph at a time. This helps ELs focus on one idea at a time while guiding them through the discourse structure of the essay and each paragraph.
- Modeled writing. The teacher is consistently modeling written English for the students. English learners visually see what persuasive writing looks like in action. They see how to write out their ideas into complete and coherent sentences.
- Persuasive writing transition sheet. Providing ELs with the language of persuasion and modeling how to use it is important. This helps strengthen their argument and develop academic language.

The opening text of this chapter on school uniforms was written by Elias, a Spanish-speaking EL in fifth grade. He was at an "intermediate fluency stage" of second language acquisition when he wrote his essay on school uniforms. The essay was written as a result of the above instructional writing sequence. Figure 4.4 was Elias's first persuasive writing piece during their first unit of study in language arts. In reading his initial piece you'll notice that Elias began his essay like a narrative. This is common in fifth grade because students are not very familiar with persuasive writing. They spend the first four years in school writing mostly narrative and expository texts. Therefore, when writing persuasive text for the first time they often apply what they know about narratives to telling a story about a time they tried to convince someone of something. It becomes a recount of a persuasive event, but not a persuasive essay. Once Elias was taught how to structure his argument in a typical persuasive essay structure, his improvement was amazing. From the draft in Figure 4.4 to what we saw from him in his piece on school uniforms to open this chapter, we can see how important it is to scaffold the elements of persuasive writing. On the rubric I presented to the students, see Figure 4.5, Persuasive Essay Rubric, Elias showed full competency in his ability to write a persuasive essay by the end of our instructional writing sequence. However, there is still a lot of room for growth; from this point the teacher can begin to work on different types of supports for his argument. In addition, the rubric presented is only one example of sharing our expectations with students for the given writing task. The sample provided only demonstrates competency. It does not present a grading scale. I have found some wonderful persuasive writing rubrics by Adele Fiderer in her many books available on reading and writing rubrics and checklists.

Steven Graham and Karen R. Harris (2007) discuss a few fun mnemonics for writing persuasive text. The DARE strategy reminds students about the key elements for developing an argument. "DARE reminds them to check to see if they included these four parts: **D**evelop a topic sentence; **A**dd supporting ideas; **R**eject arguments for the other side; **E**nd with a conclusion" (Graham & Harris, 2007, p. 138). This is a nice reminder for students who DARE to persuade.

TYPES OF SUPPORTS	DESCRIPTION	LANGUAGE CUES
HYPOTHETICAL SITUATION	PROVIDES THE READER WITH A DIFFERENT POINT OF VIEW. MAKES THEM THINK ABOUT WHAT MIGHT BE/MIGHT HAPPEN IF (YOUR ARGUMENT) WAS NOT SUPPORTED.	WHAT IF . . . SUPPOSE THAT . . . LET'S SUPPOSE THAT . . . IT IS POSSIBLE THAT . . .
PERSONAL EXPERIENCE	YOU PROVIDE A FIRSTHAND ACCOUNT OF THE IMPACT/EFFECT OF THE ARGUMENT.	PERSONALLY I FIND THAT . . . WHEN I WAS . . . I . . . I CAN REMEMBER A TIME WHEN . . . ON MANY OCCASIONS I . . .
USING ANALOGIES	FINDING SIMILARITIES BETWEEN TWO OR MORE OBJECTS, IDEAS, OR ARGUMENTS WHEN THEY ARE OTHERWISE QUITE DIFFERENT.	THOUGH IT MAY NOT SEEM CLEAR, . . .IS CLOSELY RELATED TO . . . AT FIRST GLANCE . . . AND . . . MAY SEEM VERY DIFFERENT; HOWEVER, . . .
RESEARCH	PRESENT RESEARCH THAT HAS BEEN CONDUCTED ON A SIMILAR TOPIC/ARGUMENT TO SUPPORT YOUR FINDINGS. OR YOU CAN CRITIQUE POOR RESEARCH TO GIVE STRENGTH TO YOURS.	THESE FINDINGS WERE SIMILAR TO WHAT . . . (YEAR) FOUND IN THEIR RESEARCH ON . . . IN . . . (YEAR), THE RESEARCHERS TRIED TO SHOW THAT . . . HOWEVER, THESE FINDINGS ARE SIMILAR TO . . .
ANALYSIS	YOU CAN BREAK THE ARGUMENT DOWN INTO ITS SIMPLEST PARTS TO BUILD YOUR POINT.	LOOKING CLOSELY AT . . . YOU CAN SEE THAT . . .
COMPARISONS	COMPARISONS WITH OTHERS WHO HAVE SHARED A SIMILAR ARGUMENT OR YOU CAN USE OPPOSING VIEWPOINTS TO GIVE STRENGTH TO YOUR ARGUMENT.	SIMILAR TO . . . AS SEEN IN . . . LOOKING CLOSELY AT THE WORK OF . . . YOU CAN SEE THAT WE SHARE SIMILAR . . . AS OPPOSED TO . . . UNLIKE . . . . . . FAILED TO SHOW THAT . . . WHEREAS MY RESEARCH FOUND THAT . . .
QUOTES	DIRECT QUOTES FROM LEADING EXPERTS.	PROVIDE MODELS FOR PUNCTUATING AND REFERENCING QUOTES.
EXAMPLES	PROVIDES DESCRIPTIVE EVIDENCE.	FOR EXAMPLE . . . AS AN EXAMPLE . . .
COUNTERARGUMENTS	STATE THE CONS AGAINST YOUR ARGUMENT. WHAT MIGHT THE OPPOSITION SAY AGAINST YOUR POSITION.	OTHERS MAY ARGUE THAT . . . THE OPPOSITION MIGHT BELIEVE THAT . . . BUT . . . AS OPPOSED TO (YOUR ARGUMENT) OTHERS MAY THINK THAT . . .; HOWEVER, . . .
FACTS	INFORMATION THAT YOU CAN PROVE IS TRUE NOT JUST A GENERAL TRUTH. MUST BE SUPPORTED WITH LITERATURE OR RESEARCH.	IT IS A FACT THAT . . . AS A MATTER OF FACT . . . ACCORDING TO . . .
CLARIFYING KEY VOCABULARY	PROVIDE SUFFICIENT APPOSITION OF KEY WORDS THAT DIRECTLY SUPPORT YOUR ARGUMENT.	THE MEANING OF KEY VOCABULARY WORDS IS SET OFF BY COMMAS TYPICALLY DIRECTLY FOLLOWING THE WORD. FOR EXAMPLE, "THE DERMATOLOGIST, SKIN DOCTOR, DETERMINED THE CAUSE OF THE NEW DARK SPOTS ON HER FACE."
STATISTICS	THE COLLECTION, ANALYSIS, INTERPRETATION, AND PRESENTATION OF DATA IN NUMERICAL FORM.	(NUMERIC VALUE) PERCENT OF PEOPLE SURVEYED AGREED THAT . . . ACCORDING TO . . . (NUMERIC VALUE) PERCENT OF THE POPULATION . . . . . . OUT OF . . . PEOPLE QUESTIONED BELIEVED THAT . . .

Figure 4.3 Ways to Support an Argument

8-14-03

<u>Students should choose Teams</u>

I am going to be writing why students should choose teams. I am going to write a good, interesting and persuasive story. I am going to have plenty of ideas because I want you people to know why students should choose teams.

I think the students should choose teams because they might make it more exciting. Also it could help them so that when they grow up they could make teams or they could become coaches. If they choose teams they could pick their own friends.

If the students choose teams that will make them act more grown up. Also if the students choose teams they wont pick their (enemyes). Also students should choose teams because if teachers choose teams they might be bossing the students around. If the students choose teams they will pick someone that they could count on, that will do teamwork and that will pass the ball. Those are all my ideas why students should choose teams.

Figure 4.4   Elias's First Persuasive Piece

INTRODUCTION	CATCHY OPENING—PULLS IN THE READER
	THESIS IS PRESENTED
	MAIN ARGUMENTS/REASONS TO SUPPORT THE THESIS ARE STATED
BODY	EACH SUPPORTING PARAGRAPH CONTAINS A FOCUSED REASON TO SUPPORT THE THESIS
	EACH SUPPORTING PARAGRAPH INCLUDES STRONG EVIDENCE TO SUPPORT THE MAIN ARGUMENT
	VARIED FORMS OF SUPPORT ARE INCLUDED: FOR EXAMPLE, PERSONAL EXPERIENCE, FACTS, QUOTES, STATISTICS
	COUNTERARGUMENTS ARE ADDRESSED
CONCLUSION	THE THESIS IS RESTATED
	STRONG FINAL SENTENCE WITH A CLEAR MESSAGE
ORGANIZATION	ESSAY FOLLOWS A LOGICAL PROGRESSION OF IDEAS
	PARAGRAPHS FLOW FROM ONE IDEA TO THE NEXT USING TRANSITION WORDS
	MAIN IDEAS AND ARGUMENTS ARE GROUPED TOGETHER TO MAINTAIN THE FOCUS FOR EACH PARAGRAPH
GRAMMAR, USAGE, AND MECHANICS	GRAMMAR IS NOT DISTRACTING
	APPROPRIATE PUNCTUATION IS USED
	SENTENCES ARE COMPLETE AND COHERENT

Figure 4.5   Persuasive Essay Rubric

PERSUASIVE GENRES

Students are asked to write persuasive text through a variety of genres. Specifically they are asked to create persuasive letters, persuasive compositions and interpretive responses to literature. Each of these three genres of persuasive writing requires students to take a position, take a stance on an issue or idea, and present thoughtful and thorough supports. The instructional writing sequence presented for writing a persuasive essay can be used when preparing students to write a persuasive letter as well. When writing literary essays, often referred to as responses to literature, there are similarities to the persuasive composition, but it will differ in its types of supports.

Literary Essays

A literary essay is a reflection of a student's interpretation of a read text. It involves the development of a thesis statement that encapsulates their understanding of a personal point of view. Once the thesis has been developed the student will write their essay using text support throughout. The argument must stay grounded in the text, using the text to back up their point of view. As noted in the California Language Arts standards, a well written response to literature should:

- Develop interpretations exhibiting careful reading, understanding, and insight.
- Organize interpretations around several clear ideas, premises, or images from the literary work.
- Justify interpretations through sustained use of examples and textual evidence.
- Connect the student's own responses to the writer's techniques and to specific textual references.
- Draw supported inferences about the effects of a literary work on its audience.
- Support judgments through references to the text, other works, other authors, or to personal knowledge.

The use of the text as both the basis from which the argument is developed and the primary source of support helps ELs. They will have had the opportunity to read and talk about the piece of literature, thus developing the background knowledge necessary to write the composition. What they will then need is guidance on how to properly structure their essay in a coherent and comprehensive manner. To help ELs understand the discourse structure for writing a literary essay, I engage them in a series of mini-lessons that include:

- The development of the thesis—What is your opinion?
- Determining three key ideas to support their thesis.
- Identifying text support. Using the graphic organizer provided in Resource V: Text Support, the students spend time reviewing the text finding evidence to support their position.
- Organizing their ideas. Using the graphic organizer provided in Resource W: Planning a Literary Essay, the students will plan their essay.
- Writing the essay. The students are guided paragraph by paragraph as they write a first draft.

After completing a shared reading of the book *The Thief Lord* by Cornelia Funke, I had my sixth graders write a literary essay based on their interpretation of the main character, Scipio. The following introduction and supporting paragraph comes from a literary essay written by a sixth grade student, who at the time was at an "intermediate fluency" level of second language acquisition. I have used this piece as a model when teaching the introduction and how it transitions into the first supporting paragraph. I point out to the students how the fist idea in the thesis statement connects directly to the opening sentence of paragraph #2. Though he can continue to tighten his examples and analysis, because of the scaffolding provided, his ideas are logical and clear. With the structure in place it is easier to work through the development of the rest of his essay.

Chris, 1999

Never Grow Up Too Fast

The Thief Lord, by Cornelia Funke is a story about two brothers, Prosper and Boniface, who runaway to Venice after their mother's death. They meet a boy named Scipio who helps them survive on the streets of Venice. Prosper, twelve, is trying to protect his little five year old brother Bo from having to live with their mean aunt Ester. Ester wants to find the boys so she can send Prosper to an orphanage and only keep Bo. But the deeper story is about the desire to grow up too fast. Scipio, *the thief lord,* was a wealthy boy who was tired of being told what to do. He spent his time pretending to be a thief to impress a group of street kids, including Prosper and Bo. These kids became his best friends and ultimately his chance to escape his controlling father. Scipio wanted to become a grown up so he could live his own life and not have to do everything his father says. His wish to become older as soon as possible was evident in his control over the street kids, his quest to find the magical merry-go-round, and his idea to become a detective.

One day Scipio met a group of street kids, Mosca, Hornet, and Riccio, looking for a place to stay. Scipio pretended to be a runaway named *the thief lord* and the four became great friends. The group respected Scipio because he took care of them. He put them up in one of his father's old, rundown movie theatres and would supposedly steal things from rich houses late in the evening for the three to sell for money to survive. He would be gone for days and his friends simply thought he was on an adventure. *The thief lord* would stay at his parents' house and when he had a chance he would sneak out with some of his fathers belongings. These were the things he said he stole. He told his friends never to question his whereabouts and he would send them on missions for him. Scipio was very demanding and gave the group orders for carrying out missions for him. He was very sneaky because he didn't want anyone to find out he was actually rich. It also made him feel grown up because he was able to order the street kids around. He was the boss and all the street kids looked up to him.

To help students write an effective literary essay, they need time to work with the text. Careful planning on how to support students as they research the text for evidence to support their thesis is important. Once they have collected enough information from the text, it is time to make it their own by providing their interpretation of the text. This level of analysis can be difficult for ELs to express in a second language. For this reason, helping them first express the language of the text in their own words with a partner can facilitate comprehension. They can then use quotes to support their language as they develop their thesis throughout the essay. The key will be in giving ELs time to discuss and understand the text before planning their literary essay.

MAKING IT PUBLIC

Students are traditionally asked to present their persuasive arguments in a standard essay. However, to really help them understand the role of persuasive writing in their daily lives, they need opportunities to publish their work in more authentic ways. Persuasive writing is such a prevalent type of writing in children's lives. The key is to use what they know and are exposed to as a motivation for writing persuasive texts. We do not want to turn students off from persuasive writing by always demanding the five-plus paragraph essay. Figure 4.6, Publishing Persuasive Text, provides some ideas on how students might get a chance to publish persuasion in ways that will inspire them to want to write.

Persuasive compositions	Advertisement
Editorials	Political cartoons
Classified ads	Monologues
Letter to the editor	Commercials
Proposals	Persuasive letters/friendly letter
Complaint letter/business letter	Business pitch (poster/billboard)
Advice column	Travel brochures
Speeches	
Response to literature	
Book jackets	
Movie trailer	
Book and movie reviews	

Figure 4.6   Publishing Persuasive Text

CONCLUSION

Children are surrounded with examples of persuasive writing. They see, hear, and read varied sources of information that try to influence their thoughts and actions. We need to capitalize on these experiences with persuasion and encourage students to voice their beliefs and opinions. Stirring their emotions to prepare for persuasive writing will motivate students to want to write. Once they have selected a position and made a statement, they need explicit instruction on how to organize their ideas effectively. The power of an argument is in the presentation of supporting evidence and opinions. Students need guidance on how to craft an argument, the types of supports they can use, and how to captivate their audience. What makes persuasive writing even more appealing to students is the real-world application. They can create those same advertisements, editorials, and commercials that influenced their opinions in the first place.

RESOURCES FOR TEACHING PERSUASIVE WRITING

6 Tricks to Student Persuasive Writing Success, Mark Diamond

How to Win Friends and Influence People for Teen Girls, Donna Dale Carnegie

Why We Must Run With Scissors: Voice Lesson in Persuasive Writing, Barry Lane, Gretchen Bernabei

Writing About Reading: From Book Talk to Literary Essays, Grades 3-8, Janet Angelillo

Earrings!, Judith Viorst

I Wanna Iguana, Karen Kaufman Orloff

The Perfect Pet, Margie Palatini

The Principal's New Clothes, Stephanie Calmenson

Poetry 5

Photo by Eugenia Mora-Flores.

Once upon the middle of the day
Seven Dwarfs went out to play

A woman came by
Just to say hi
But then decided to stay

She cooked and she cleaned
But could never be seen
Or the witch would
  make her pay

She hated Ms. White
Because of her sight
And ordered her out of the way

Away working hard
Till the sky became starred
The seven head home for bed

Meanwhile from afar
The witch talks to her wall
And aha! Ms. White is not dead

She stirred with emotion
With a fearful notion
For she longed to be the best

Awake the next day
The dwarfs on their way
And Snow White stayed home to rest

Much more than a treat
Ms. White was so sweet
Although a bit naïve

An old lady came by
Ms. White gave a sigh
For she was one who believed

Hiking on home
To a chant of Hi-Ho
The Dwarfs were full of shame

Crying and Crying
They were trying
But Snow White just
    stayed the same

But look here he comes
Could he be the one
To rid them of this blame

A kiss to the fairest
The witch was embarrassed
For they were destined to be

Snow White and her prince
Together since
The end as you can see
—Eugenia Mora, 1990

UNDERSTANDING POETRY

About a year ago I was cleaning out some old boxes that included homework, projects, papers, and exams I had written when I was in school. Within these boxes I found some old poetry I had written. The above poem was one of my many finds. It was a poem I wrote in the ninth grade. I can remember our assignment was to write a poem about a fairy tale to submit to *Teen* magazine, a popular magazine at the time. Our teacher wanted us to experience writing for publication. I can't remember why we were told to write about a fairy tale because when I re-read my rejection letter from the magazine, it very nicely stated that it was not a good fit for their current issue but will consider it for the future. The reason I share it with you now is to demonstrate the endless possibilities of poetry. Poetry transcends literary and written genres in unique ways. You can write narrative, expository, and persuasive poems. They can be about any topic while at the same time follow specific poetic forms. Poetry is a type of written text that can appeal to all students because it allows them to play with language. They can manipulate word meanings and challenge written English by breaking syntactic rules.

Poetry is in itself a study of language. Marjorie R. Hancock (2003) in her book *A Celebration of Literature and Response* (2nd edition) does a wonderful job of explaining the connection between poetry and language. She states, "The elements of poetry are essentially language related . . . language, in all its glory and with all its propensity to capture objects, emotions and thoughts" (p. 109). Poetry provides the medium for exploring purposeful, original uses of language.

She goes on to express the elements of poetry and their relationship to spoken and written language (p. 111):

- Rhythm: includes the flow of language and how it makes the words dance off the page. It creates movement.
- Rhyme: adds to the musical element of poetry through the selection of similar word sounds that help create rhythm.
- Imagery: selected language can create a sensory experience for the reader or listener.
- Figurative language: includes the literary devices used to create images in a poem. They include similes, metaphors, personification, and idioms. Figure 5.1, Literary and Poetic Devices, provides a more descriptive list of literary and poetic devices.
- Shape and spacing: involves the arrangement of the words including stanzas, indentations, line length, centering, and margins. In the eyes of many children it is the shape and spacing decisions that make something a poem.

For a child to write a poem it takes a considerable amount of time selecting the right language, written in the right way to convey an intended meaning. Poetry writing involves a great deal of critical thinking and decision making. For many of us it is a scary thing. Where some may think they are not good writers, many think they are not poets. But poetry is about the beauty of language, and we all have and use language, so technically we are all poets. It is the way we CHOOSE to use our words. It is how we say them, in the order we say them, how we leave words out, or interrupt a statement to convey an idea or emotion.

It wasn't until I read the book *Awakening the Heart* by Georgia Heard that I realized I too can teach my students to become poets. In her book she talks about the need for students to understand poetry to write it. It is an analytic approach whereby students are asked to begin by just listening to the poetry around them: Listen for great words, the music in someone's voice, the language of their family and friends. Teachers can be purposeful about this by making it a morning routine to read a poem out loud to their students. Students then begin to read poetry and make connections to their own thoughts and emotions. A teacher can enhance this experience by finding poems that relate to the students both academically and personally. For example, third graders would enjoy Jack Prelutsky's poetry in *It's Raining Pigs and Noodles* and *For Laughing Out Loud: Poems to Tickle Your Funnybone*. He writes about everyday topics of school and home in a very comical way. With my sixth to eighth graders I read from books entitled *Cool Salsa* (1995) and *Red Hot Salsa: Bilingual Poems on Being Young and Latino in the United States* edited by Lori Carlson. There are many poems related to fitting in and soul searching, very relevant to my students' adolescent experience. Once the students have had a chance to immerse themselves in poems of all types, they are more prepared to think through the writing of a poem. Figure 5.2, Lessons to Support Writing Poetry, provides a series of lessons that help to facilitate the writing of poetry. They are not meant to be sequential; they are just some ideas to explore poetry with your students before having them write their own.

POETIC DEVICES	DESCRIPTION	EXAMPLE
SIMILE	A COMPARISON BETWEEN TWO OBJECTS USING THE WORDS "LIKE" OR "AS."	HER SMILE IS *LIKE* A SUNSET.
METAPHOR	A COMPARISON OF TWO UNLIKE OBJECTS INTENDING TO CLARIFY THE MEANING OF ONE OF THEM. OFTEN "TO BE" VERBS ARE USED TO MAKE THE COMPARISON, E.G., "IS" "WAS."	CLOUDS *ARE* PILLOWS OF FEATHERS THAT OVERSHADOW US.
ASSONANCE	THE REPETITION OF VOWEL SOUNDS.	*AMY ATE* A *LATE* SNACK.
CONSONANCE	THE REPETITION OF CONSONANT SOUNDS. UNLIKE ALLITERATION IT CAN HAPPEN ANYWHERE IN THE WORD.	THE *BIRD HEARD* A CRACKLE *BEHIND* THE *SHED.*
ALLITERATION	THE REPETITION OF INITIAL CONSONANT SOUNDS. TYPICALLY SEQUENTIAL AND WITHIN A LINE OF POETRY.	SILLY *SALLY SAT* UP *STRAIGHT* AND TALL. SHE *LOOKED,* AND *LISTENED LIKE* A HAWK.
ONOMATOPOEIA	WORDS USED TO IMITATE SOUND.	BOOM! MEOW.
PERSONIFICATION	GIVING HUMAN-LIKE QUALITIES OR CHARACTERISTICS TO ANIMALS, IDEAS, OR INANIMATE OBJECTS.	THE *CLOCK STARED* AT US AS WE WAITED FOR THE TRAIN TO ARRIVE.
RHYME SCHEME	THE SEQUENCE IN WHICH RHYMES OCCUR.	THE HOUSE SMELLED OF *FLOWERS* AS SHE WAITED BY THE <u>DOOR.</u> HE ENTERED FROM *SHOWERS* HIS CLOTHES DRIPPING TO THE <u>FLOOR.</u>
RHYME	THE REPETITION OF SIMILAR SOUNDS.	THE BOY SAT IN *BED* WITH THE COVERS OVER *HEAD* HIS FACE TURNED *RED* IT WAS A NIGHT OF *DREAD*

Figure 5.1   Literary and Poetic Devices

Found Poems

Found poems are very popular and can be created in a variety of ways. They are considered *found* poems because it was "not intended as a poem, but is so declared by its founder" (Padgett, 2000, p. 79). Here are three suggestions for creating a found poem:

Student voices: In this method, the teacher will listen to the students throughout the school day and jot down some words, phrases, or sounds she hears. She then takes what she has heard and creates a poem out of it. The example below was a found poem I created from my students' voices when I taught middle school in New York City:

Here we go

I forgot it

I wish he could have called

We can't control ourselves

Not again

It's so you

When is this over

We made it

The bell?

Hata mañana

Late

It ended up being somewhat of a chronology of their day; from the morning bell to goodbye (hata mañana) at the end of the day. You can organize your students' language in any way that makes sense to you. You then share the poem with your students. It is a way for them to see that poetry comes from their own language, and it can be created to the liking of the poet.

Our words: Similar to the method in *student voices* this found poem will be created by using the language that is heard throughout the day. But in this case the students will be responsible for jotting down words or phrases they hear their family use at home to organize into a found poem. They come to school ready to share their poem. I call this *our words* because they belong to the student and their family. So when they share they say, "This poem was created using *our* words, the words of my family."

The two samples below were written by third graders. What is great about found poems is seeing how the students decide to craft their poem. They are not given directions on how to organize the language they recorded from home. They use their own background knowledge of poetry and their own creativity. In the first example, Figure 5.2a, Ana used repetition to bring out the emphasis of always being told to do her homework. She even shows some negotiation before giving in. In the second example, Figure 5.2b, Edgar does something different with the language he heard at home. His poem shows a change in tone from negative to positive.

Figure 5.2   Lessons to Support Writing Poetry

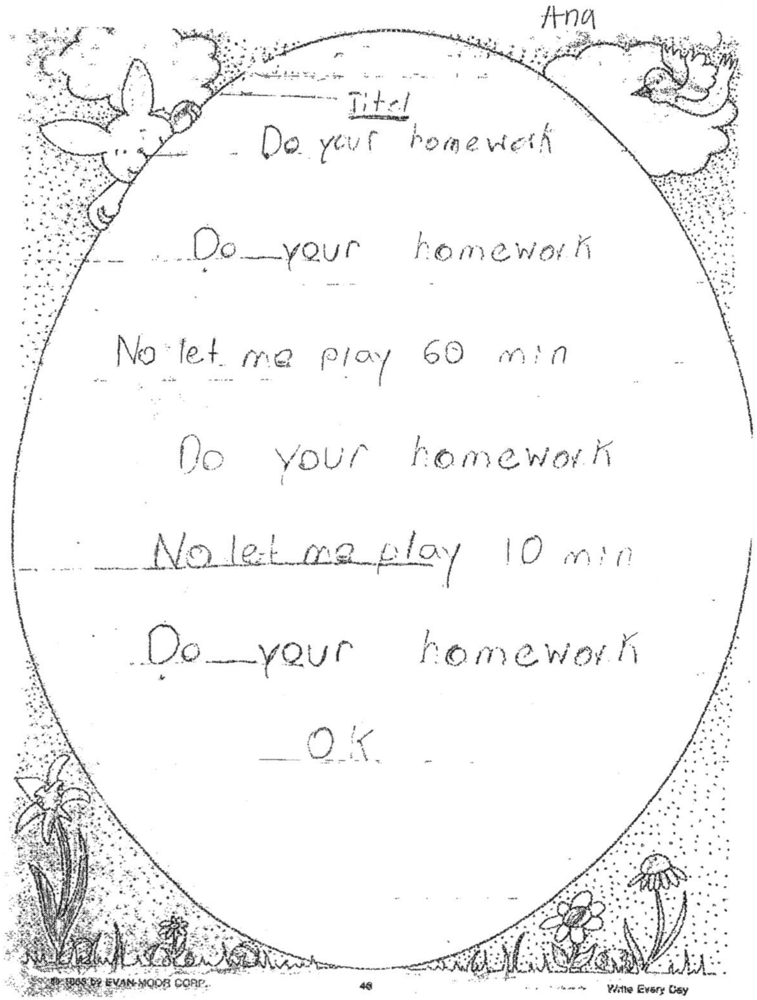

Figure 5.2a Ana's Found Poem

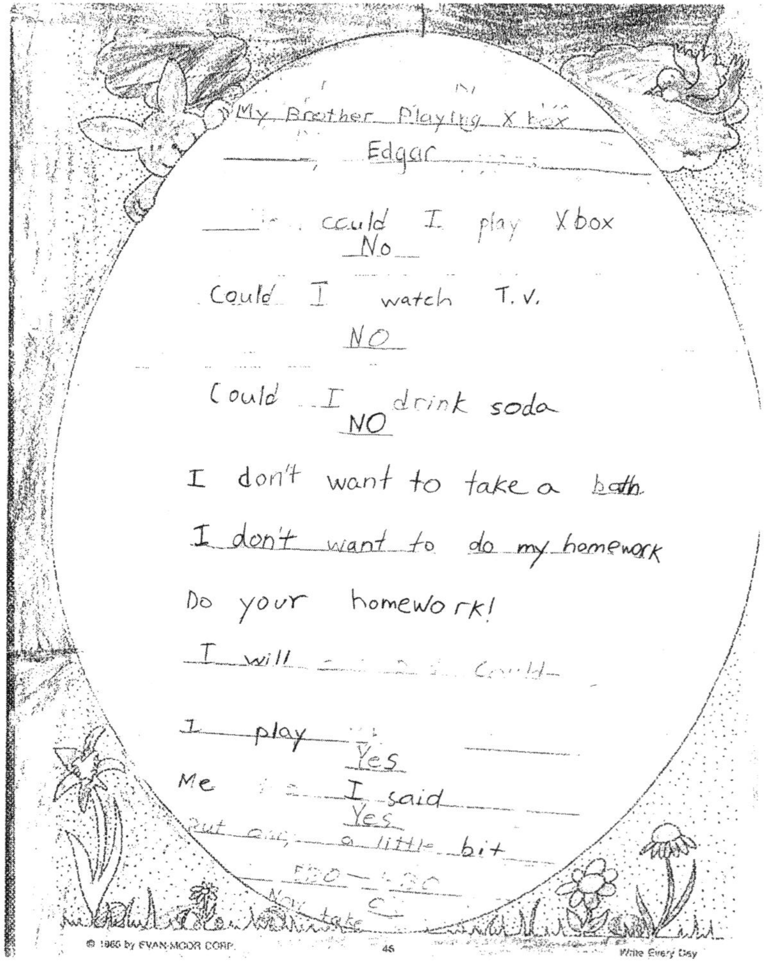

Figure 5.2b Edgar's Found Poem

Their words: In this found poem we use the words of authors. So we are not using *our* words anymore, but *theirs*. Ask students to select a word, phrase, or sentence from a text you provide that they like for whatever reason. Perhaps they liked the way it sounded, it made them think of something in their life or they just liked the word choice. The text you use does not have to be a poem; it can be any text. You will then put the students into groups of five. Each student will use the language they selected (from the poem or text) and combine it with their group members to create a poem. You'll want to share the following with the students:

- Every group member must contribute the language they selected from the poem or text. Whether it is a sentence, a word, or a phrase each person can only contribute one.
- They may use the contributions of each member more than once to craft the group poem, so they can use repetition.
- They can organize their poem in any way they choose.
- They will have to decide how they will perform their poem in front of the class.

As each group shares out their poem, ask them to explain "how" they created their poem. What was their process? You'll want to record each group's crafting techniques shared. This shows students that "how" you organize your words is purposeful, and it can convey a different rhythm and often different meaning.

Making a Connection

I learned this strategy from Georgia Heard in *Awakening the Heart*. Before the students come into class, tape a poem on each of their desks. As they walk in to the classroom, inform them that there are poems on each desk and they are to walk around the room and read the poems. When they read one that speaks to them, that they connect to in some way, they are to sit at that desk. Once everyone has a place to sit they do a quickwrite that expresses why they selected their poem. This activity helps students start to create meaning from poetry. In using this strategy I found it helpful to tape extra poems to open seats in the class to give all students a chance to make a connection to a poem, not just end up with the leftovers. In addition, I was sure to find poems that I thought would resonate with the students.

Listening Walk

This strategy was inspired by the children's book *The Listening Walk* by Paul Showers. I wanted my students to learn to listen to the rhythm of sounds. I start by asking my students to take their writing journals with them as we take a tour of the school. As we walk around the school I stop them on occasion and ask them to just listen. I instruct them to try and isolate sounds they hear in their environment in that moment. After making them listen for about one minute, I tell them to write down what it was they heard. They get about another minute to write. We then continue walking, stopping on occasion to just listen and then write what we heard. Once the students have had a chance to capture at least six sounds, we return to the classroom. The students are then asked to create a sound poem using a very simple structure of:

1. The . . . goes . . .
2. and the . . . goes . . .
3. The . . . goes . . .
4. and the . . . goes . . .

They read them out loud to a partner. This can lead to a lesson on onomatopoeia.

In My Words

This strategy is a very popular strategy used with students to help them process, in their own words, challenging poetry. I learned this strategy when reading Janet Allen's book *Yellow Brick Roads: Shared and Guided Paths to Independent Reading 4–12*. In her chapter on reading aloud to students, there is an example of a modern-day version of Romeo and Juliet. I realized what a great activity this would be for

(Continued)

(Continued)

students as they prepare for understanding the often difficult language of poetry. I break up my students into groups of five. After reading a poem out loud to the class, I give each group a stanza. They are required to rewrite their stanza using *their* own language. Once each group rewrites their stanza, we re-read the poem out loud as each group takes its turn to read its rewritten stanza. I prefer to let students work together on the stanzas because they can help one another process the original poem.

Poetry in Motion

When I lived in New York City I had the pleasure of enjoying Poetry in Motion. They are simply short poems that are posted in the buses and subways. It was a nice way to pass the time on those lengthy rides. So I decided to put this idea into practice with my students. I asked each student to select a short poem (four to six lines) from our class poetry books. Each student was given a poster board to write his or her poem and illustrate it. We then asked the principal for permission to post them all over the school. This way the entire school was able to read great poetry as they were in motion throughout their day. As a class you can engage students in a discussion about where in the school certain poems should be placed depending on the theme or message of the poem. This helps the students interpret poetry and its meaning in a way that makes sense to them and they can relate to.

These activities are a few ways of introducing students to poetry. They help students begin to understand the purpose and elements of poetry. I encourage you to read Georgia Heard's books on poetry. She has truly become my mentor in teaching poetry to children.

POETIC FORMS

As teachers of poetry we are empowered by the many poetic forms for teaching poetry. They provide us a variety of ways of thinking about poetry. They give us more tools for teaching children the many ways a poem can be written. We often wonder if the use of forms is stifling students' creativity as poets, thinking we should teach them to develop their own style and form, but when you take a closer look at poetic forms, there is a great deal of room for creativity and individuality. They are actually not as simple as filling in the blanks; they involve a great deal of decision making and clever uses of language. But what does make the poetic forms especially helpful for English learners (ELs) is the well-defined structure. And they will still have the flexibility to use *their* language, including their primary language, when writing within the poetic form. Throughout the rest of this chapter I will be sharing some popular poetic forms for exploring poetry with students. These will include a look at haiku, cinquains, diamantes, acrostic poems, and limericks.

Haiku

A haiku is a traditional Japanese poem. Though it has changed over time, today it includes a seventeen-syllable verse form consisting of three metrical units of five, seven, and five syllables. Haiku written in different languages can follow a variety of different patterns and themes; however, in a true sense, it remains true to the basic five, seven, five syllable structure and can be written about any topic or theme. It can often shed new light on a common daily situation or idea. In addition, it is common when writing a haiku to include a seasonal theme. This is referred to as a *kigo*, a season word, indicating in which season the poem is set. Though its form seems rather simple, the thought and reflection involved in creating and interpreting a haiku is complex. The haiku below was written and published by Hector, one of my seventh graders, during a study of Puerto Rico in Spanish class.

> *But it's who I am*
>
> *Wrong, we never hear of it*
>
> *Thank you for caring*

I remember when Hector shared his haiku with the class it really made an impact on me as a teacher. That year I taught seventh and eighth grade Spanish, and the majority of my students' families were from Puerto Rico and the Dominican Republic. I made a decision to supplement the curriculum on Spain with a study of Puerto Rico and the Dominican Republic. One day in the middle of class Hector called out, "I don't get it Ms., why hasn't anybody ever taught us about this before. This is my people, this is who I am." For the first time Hector felt that he was a part of our class, that he was valued in our learning. It was a powerful moment for me as a relatively new teacher. Hector made me understand the value of taking students outside the box, outside of the curriculum, to truly learn how to become critical thinkers. At the end of the year I received a wonderful letter from one of my parents that read, "You made the students keep reading and thinking after the books were closed, thank you." I kept that letter and it became my purpose as a teacher, to teach children to think beyond the text, beyond my words and think for themselves, to help students truly become lifelong learners. What this poem further made me realize, in retrospect, is the power of writing. It gives students a voice. And for those who may become discouraged as ELs to express their voice in long compositions, they feel empowered to share it through the simple language, yet complex meaning, of poetry.

Cinquain

A cinquain is a poem with five lines. The word cinquain is French meaning "a grouping of five." These five lines can be developed based on the number of words per line or the number of syllables. In either case it should build up to a climax in the last line.

The word pattern includes:
Line 1: one word
(noun: the subject or title of poem)
Line 2: two words (adjectives)
Line 3: three words (verbs)
Line 4: four words that relate to feelings
Line 5: one word (relates to line 1)

The syllable pattern includes:
Line 1: two syllables
Line 2: four syllables
Line 3: six syllables
Line 4: eight syllables
Line 5: two syllables

The cinquain below was written by a third grader using the word pattern. Esmeralda was at an "early production stage" of second language acquisition when she wrote this poem.

Flower

Pretty, Bright

Grow, Bloom, Die

They smell so nice

Roses

What makes form poems fun for ELs is the simplicity of the language used. As seen in the cinquain above, Esmeralda is able to craft a poem, with few words, that holds great meaning. English learners can use short statements, often single words, to convey meaning and feelings.

Diamante

The diamante is a seven-line poem that involves a gradual change from one idea to a direct opposite idea. The pattern of the diamante, based on the number of words used in each line, helps create the visual diamond shape of the poem. Similar to most poetic forms, the topic of a diamante is open to any topic or idea. An idea for writing diamantes with students is to have them work from the outside in. Have them identify their opposing ideas (line 1 and line 7), then work their way to the middle. Below you will find the components and structure of a diamante. In addition, Resource X: Diamante, provides a graphic organizer for writing a diamante.

Line 1: Noun that is an antonym of line 7

Line 2: Two adjectives to describe line 1

Line 3: Three gerunds (–ing) about line 1

Line 4: Two nouns about line 1, two nouns about line 7

Line 5: Three gerunds (–ing) about line 7

Line 6: Two adjectives to describe line 7

Line 7: Noun that is an antonym of line 1

The two diamantes below were written by fifth graders. Gabriel (Figure 5.3) was an EL at a "speech emergent" stage of second language acquisition when he wrote this poem. Allan (Figure 5.4) arrived in the United States from El Salvador at the beginning of the school year. He was at an "early production" stage of second language acquisition. What you may notice is that though both students followed the same form, Gabriel used idea nouns while Allan used concrete nouns. Gabriel is able to verbalize in English abstract concepts. Allan is knowledgeable and able to think abstractly but has not developed the English to verbalize or write his thoughts in English. If given an opportunity to write in

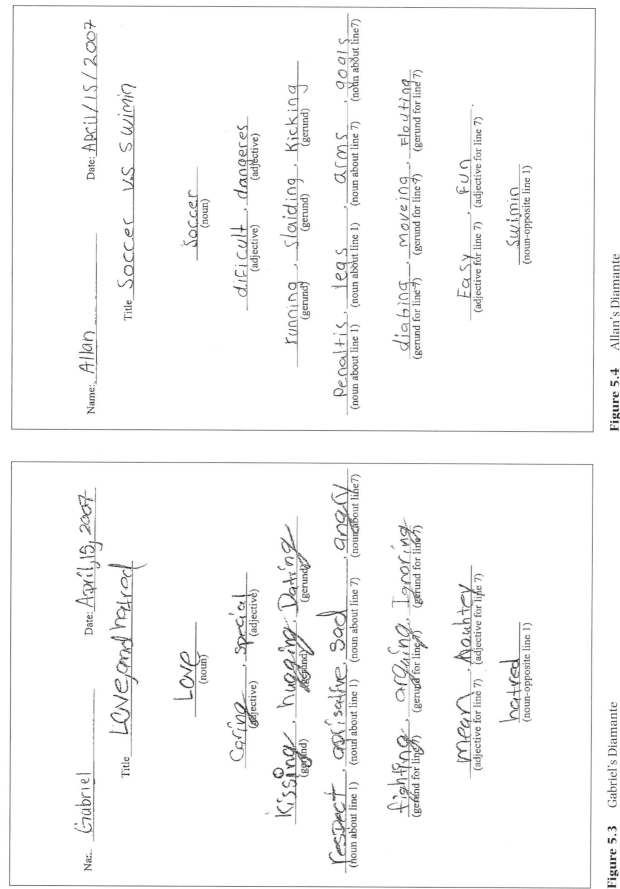

Figure 5.3 Gabriel's Diamante

Figure 5.4 Allan's Diamante

Spanish, we would see more evidence of Allan's higher order thinking skills. In this example he is showing us what he is able to produce in written English. If you look closely at Allan's spelling, you will notice that he is transferring his knowledge of Spanish phonetics when writing in English. For example, for "diving" he wrote "diabing."

Acrostic Poem

An acrostic poem is a vertical poem that begins with one word. The students can select any topic (word) from which to create their poem or it can be used as a way of writing across the curriculum. You can have students create an acrostic based on a character in a story they read or a person they are studying in history class, or it can be a vocabulary word or science concept to demonstrate their understanding of the topic in a creative way.

Once the topic, person, or word has been selected, the students will write the word vertically with one letter per line of the poem. The student then goes line by line writing out an idea, statement, or sentence related to the topic. The acrostic poem shared below in Figure 5.5, "New York," was written by Manuel, a third grader, after returning from a winter vacation in New York City. At the time Manuel was at a "speech emergent" level of second language acquisition when he wrote his acrostic poem. He explained that he really misses New York City so he wanted to write about it.

This is what I love about poetry. Children share their innermost thoughts and feelings in simple yet very meaningful ways. So many students have revealed themselves through their poetry. Regardless of the form you ask them to use to craft a poem, they always select topics that are meaningful. They make personal connections to their ideas and words.

Limericks

Limericks have always been some of my students' favorite poems to write. A limerick is a five-line poem with a particular rhyme scheme that is humorous and often nonsensical. The first, second, and fifth lines contain three beats and rhyme with each other, and the third and fourth lines contain two beats and rhyme. They don't have to, but they often begin with: There once was . . . or There was a . . . The sample below was written by a fourth grade EL at an "intermediate fluency" stage of second language acquisition.

There once was a girl with a pool,

Who thought she was so cool,

She never went in

And still stayed thin,

It was her parents rule.

Limericks can be very fun to write. Students can write limericks about a character in a novel, a historical figure, a scientist, about family and friends, or even themselves. It is a creative way to write descriptions.

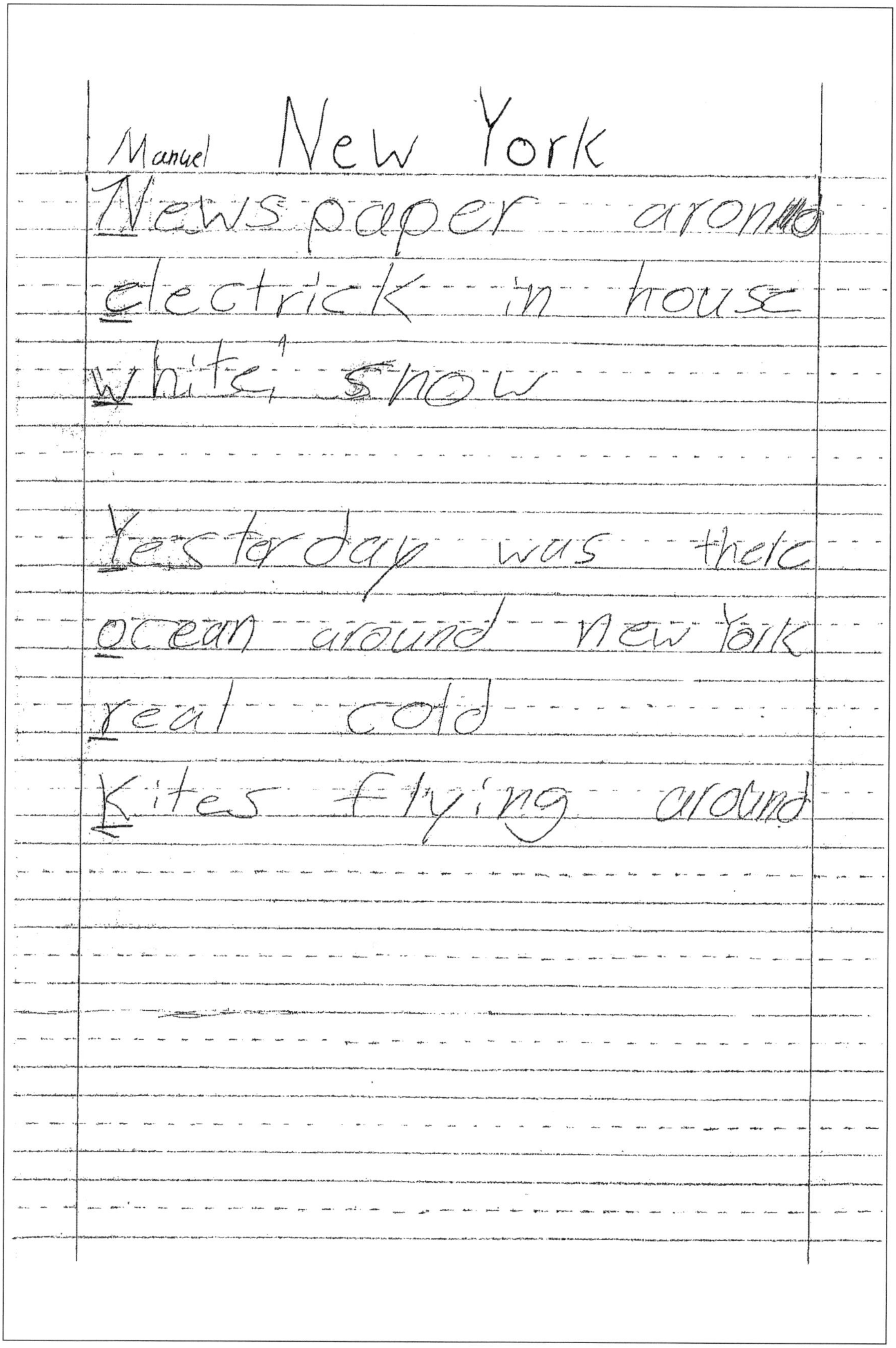

Manuel   New York

Newspaper   around
electrick   in   house
white   snow

Yesterday   was   there
ocean   around   new York
real   cold
Kites   flying   around

Figure 5.5 "New York"

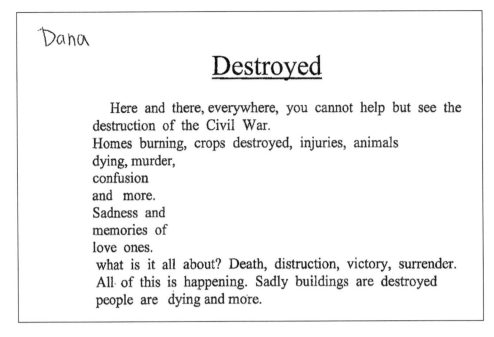

Figure 5.6 Destroyed

Free Verse Poem

Free verse poems are often misunderstood because they do not seem to have any discernable pattern. They do not typically include any particular rhyme scheme and may not even contain rhyme. It is a free flow of ideas, but the decisions the poet makes for line breaks are purposeful for the poem to flow and carry meaning. Exposing students to a variety of poems prior to allowing them the opportunity to write a free verse poem gives them the information they need to make purposeful decisions about their free-form structure. They learn how line breaks, pauses, and punctuation guide the reader to read the poem in a certain way. In addition, it helps the reader understand the meaning of the poem as the poet intended. Figure 5.6 is a free verse poem that was written by one of my sixth grade students as an assignment related to our study of the Civil War. She made many careful and non-traditional sentence/line breaks, but when you read it you can hear how she wanted it to be read. The line breaks create an emphasis on the sadness and impact of the war.

MAKING IT PUBLIC

To encourage students to write poetry, we want to think of authentic ways of "going public" with poetry. We need to think, once again, where in the real world do we see poetry? Figure 5.7, Publishing Poetry, is just a beginning in the conversation for publishing poetry. I encourage you to ask your students for other suggestions. The goal is to inspire future poets!

CONCLUSION

When writing poetry with children, give them the opportunity to explore language in its many forms first. In doing so, they will begin to see that language can be manipulated and crafted in many different ways to convey meaning. For ELs the use of poetry forms helps guide their language and thinking process. However, as with any written genre, we also want to allow them the opportunity to create their own style as writers. It is in their exploration of published poets and various forms of poetry that they can begin to develop their own craft as poets. What we want to keep in mind throughout the entire process is to value the language students bring to the writing of poetry and celebrate it!

POETRY READING (AT A LOCAL BOOKSTORE)

GREETING CARD

COFFEE MUG

POETRY ANTHOLOGY

POETRY IN MOTION

BOOKMARKS

Figure 5.7   Publishing Poetry

RESOURCES FOR TEACHING POETRY

Awakening the Heart: Exploring Poetry in Elementary and Middle School, Georgia Heard

Explore Poetry: The Reading/Writing Teacher's Companion, Donald H. Graves

For the Good of the Earth and Sun: Teaching Poetry, Georgia Heard

How to Write, Recite, and Delight in All Kinds of Poetry, Joy N. Hulme, Donna W. Guthrie

Living Voices: Multicultural Poetry in the Middle School Classroom, Jaime R. Wood

Poetry Matters: Writing a Poem From the Inside Out, Ralph Fletcher

The Teachers and Writers Handbook of Poetic Forms, Ron Padgett

Using Picture Storybooks to Teach Literary Devices, Susan Hall

Wishes, Lies and Dreams: Teaching Children to Write Poetry, Kenneth Koch, Ron Padgett

Concluding Thoughts

I am excited about the possibilities for English learners (ELs) to develop as wonderful writers. When provided the proper support, they can write well at any stage of second language acquisition. English learners need to understand what different types of written English look like and move toward their own writing style. What I try to teach all of my students and their teachers is that they have a voice, and that voice can be heard when they write. Where some students may feel comfortable talking and sharing their ideas orally, many ELs may feel intimidated. The apprehension one feels when trying to talk in a second language (L2) can be alleviated in many ways by writing in L2. Writing provides opportunities for errors. Writing allows ELs second, third, and fourth chances.

When teachers employ a process approach to writing, ELs feel their multiple attempts at writing are successful steps all writers take. In addition, when ELs have opportunities to talk with their peers along the way, it shows them that all writers struggle just the same. They see that all writers have their own decisions to make. Providing opportunities for talk is a great way to help students rehearse their ideas and practice their oral language skills. Purposeful talk around writing is part of students' development of cognitive academic language proficiencies. This talk coupled with many opportunities for ELs to see models of written English is critical.

What makes writing instruction easier than we think is the help we get from authors. Teachers are not alone. Use the many wonderful examples of published text, across genres, to teach children how to write. Think about some of your favorite fairy tales, articles, commentaries, and poems to teach children how they too can write a variety of texts. The reading and writing connection is strong when developing writers. When students read, they are exposed to how written language works and how it is organized and crafted in traditional and creative ways. When students write, they engage in reading for clarity, revision, and enjoyment. We cannot plan for writing without carefully selecting text that we will read with students through the eyes of a writer. For ELs, reading like a writer not only involves looking at the author's style and craft, but looking closely at the structure of how the text is organized for clarity and purpose. We need to be very explicit in our instructional lessons with ELs when presenting the discourse structure of different genres. They need help not only seeing how the text is written, but they need to be guided as they draft similar texts. The scaffolding of language at the draft stage of the writing process will help ELs organize their ideas. Writing traditional essays will seem less intimidating when they can take it one step at a time.

The careful attention to how a text is written and organized is only one way of writing with ELs. We have to remember that what we are working toward is personal style and independence. We provide heavy scaffolds in writing to ELs at the beginning as a way to support their language development. However, as ELs become more knowledgeable about written English and are exposed to alternative ways of writing, they will no longer need the heavy support at the drafting stage. As teachers we can determine our focus by seeing what our students are able to do as writers.

As you move forward in your work with ELs, always remember that they possess the same cognitive abilities as our English-only students. We want to be sure we maintain high standards for them as writers, while providing the proper support to help them meet those standards. Writing with ELs is truly about celebrating their language development. We want to show them that their ideas, their words, their stories are valuable and that we expect them to become great writers in English.

Resource A

Writing Personal Narratives

Name: _____   Date: _____

Personal Narratives

Event/Experience: _____

Characters		
Character	Role	Descriptors

Setting		
Sensory words that describe the setting:		
When	Where	Time of day/year/season

Plot		
Beginning	Middle	End

Resource B

Transitions for Narrative Writing

Beginning	*Middle*	*End*
At first	After a short time	Happily ever after
At the beginning	Instantly	Last of all
Once upon a time	Just when	Finally
When I was . . .	Not long after	In the end
Back when I was . . .	Previously	At last
Far away	Recently	From that day on
Long ago	All at once	Since then
There is a place	In no time	After that I never (don't)
called . . . where . . .	Suddenly	In the future
	Afterwards	
	Following that	

Beginning	*Middle*	*End*
At first	After a short time	Happily ever after
At the beginning	Instantly	Last of all
Once upon a time	Just when	Finally
When I was . . .	Not long after	In the end
Back when I was . . .	Previously	At last
Far away	Recently	From that day on
Long ago	All at once	Since then
There is a place	In no time	After that I never (don't)
called . . . where . . .	Suddenly	In the future
	Afterwards	
	Following that	

Beginning	*Middle*	*End*
At first	After a short time	Happily ever after
At the beginning	Instantly	Last of all
Once upon a time	Just when	Finally
When I was . . .	Not long after	In the end
Back when I was . . .	Previously	At last
Far away	Recently	From that day on
Long ago	All at once	Since then
There is a place	In no time	After that I never (don't)
called . . . where . . .	Suddenly	In the future
	Afterwards	
	Following that	

Resource C

Peer Revision Sheets

Title of story: _____

Opening sentence: _____

_____

Comments on opening: _____

_____

Examples of descriptive details: _____

_____

Anything your partner didn't talk about that you want to hear about or hear more about:

_____

_____

_____

Title of story: _____

Closing sentence: _____

Comments on closing: _____

State three events that lead to the ending:

1. _____

2. _____

3. _____

Anything else you think your partner should add before the ending? _____

_____

Resource D

Peer Editing Sheets

Peer Editing Sheet

Name: _____

Peer editor: _____

Title of story: _____

Grammar usage and mechanics skill (What are you looking for?): _____

Generally misspelled words:

_____

Punctuation errors to look out for: _____

_____

Peer Editing Sheet

Name: _____

Peer editor: _____

Title of story: _____

Grammar usage and mechanics skill (What are you looking for?): _____

Generally misspelled words:_____

Punctuation errors to look out for: _____

_____

Peer Editing Sheet

Name: _____

Peer editor: _____

Title of story: _____

Grammar usage and mechanics skill (What are you looking for?): _____

Generally misspelled words:

_____

Punctuation errors to look out for: _____

_____

Resource E

Looking Closely at a Fairy Tale

Name: _____   Date: _____

Name of Fairy Tale	
Opening Sentence	
Good Character(s)	
Bad/Evil Character(s)	
Magical Element(s)	
Conflict Between Good and Evil	
Threes and Sevens	
Ending Sentence	
Message or Theme	

Resource F

Comparing Fairy Tales

Name of Fairy Tale	Opening Sentence	Good Character(s)	Evil Character(s)	Magic	Conflict between Good/Evil	Threes or Sevens?	Ending	Theme or Message

Resource G

Planning for Writing

Fairy Tales

Title: _____

Setting: _____

Heroes or heroines: _____

Characteristics: _____

Magical element: _____

Villains: _____

Characteristics: _____

Magical element: _____

Beginning: _____

Problem	Solution

Ending: _____

Resource H

Planning for Writing—Tall Tales

Tall Tales

Title: _____

Problem/daily challenge: _____

Setting:

    Place: _____

    Time of day: _____

    Time of year/season: _____

    How long ago/time in history: _____

Main character: _____

Extraordinary characteristic: _____

Beginning	Middle	End
event:	problem:	hyperbole:
Event:	Event:	Event:
Hyperbole:	Event:	Funny resolution:

Resource I

Planning for Writing—Myths

Name:_____   Date: _____

Myths

Phenomenon	Setting
Characters	And that is how ... (phenomenon came to be)

Beginning (Explain the phenomenon): _____

_____

_____

Middle (How did it come to be what it is?): _____

_____

_____

_____

End (Make a statement expressing that your story is the truth about how the phenomenon came to be):

_____

_____

The moral of the story (Optional): _____

Resource J

Idea Map

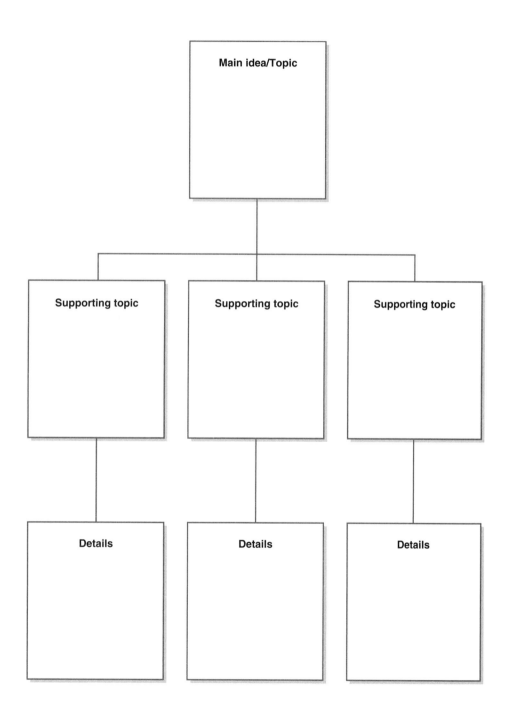

Resource K

Collecting Data

Note-Taking

Name: _____   Date: _____

Topic: _____

Text (resource)	Quote/Example/Evidence	Page number

Paraphrasing

Topic: _____

Reference: _____

Information/Quotes- page #   In your own words

Resource L

Organizing Information

Name: _____   Date: _____

Expository Essay

Topic: _____

Introduction
Opening statement (grab their attention):
First try _____
Second try _____
Third try _____
General background on your topic:
_____
_____
Three subtopics to be discussed:
1. _____
2. _____
3. _____
Supporting Paragraph
Subtopic #1: _____
Details: _____
_____
Example: _____
Quote: _____
Transition statement: _____

Supporting Paragraph

Subtopic #2: _____

Details: _____

_____

Example: _____

Quote: _____

Transition statement: _____

Supporting Paragraph

Subtopic #3: _____

Details: _____

_____

Example: _____

Quote: _____

Transition statement: _____

Conclusion

Restate the topic: _____

Three subtopics: _____

Concluding thought: _____

Writing a Paragraph

Topic sentence:

_____

_____

Supporting details:

1. _____

2. _____

3. _____

4. _____

Concluding or transition sentence: _____

_____

_____

_____

Writing a Paragraph

Topic sentence:

_____

_____

Supporting details:

1. _____

2. _____

3. _____

4. _____

Concluding or transition sentence: _____

_____

Interview Protocol

Interview Protocol: Biographies

1. What is your full name?_____

Childhood

1. When and where were you born? _____
2. Where did you live as a child? _____
3. What was your life like as a kid? What kind of things did you like to do?

   _____
   _____

4. Did you go to school? Where? _____
5. What did you enjoy most about your childhood?

   _____

6. Any fun, funny, or interesting thing happen to you when you were a kid?

   _____

Teen/Young Adult

1. What do you remember life being like when you were a teenager?

   _____

2. What were some of the challenges as a teenager?

   _____

3. Did you have any role models? What did you want to be when you got older?

   _____

4. Anything interesting or exciting happen to you when you were a teenager?

   _____

Adult

1. What do you do for a living? _____
2. What were some hardships in your life?_____
3. Did you get married and have a family?_____

4. What have you accomplished in your life that you would like to be known for?

   _____

5. Was there anything interesting happening in the world at the time?

   _____

6. Is there anything about your life you would change? _____

   _____

7. Is there anything else you would like to tell me about yourself?

   _____
   _____

Resource N

Peer Revision Sheet
for Expository Writing

Name of the writer: _____

Topic: _____

Opening sentence: _____

_____

Comments on opening: _____

_____

Is there evidence of the following (check all that apply to their writing)?

Maintained a focus/stayed on topic: ☐

Logical sequence and easy to follow: ☐

Transition words guide the sequence: ☐

Is the information from one paragraph to the next balanced? ☐

Anything your partner didn't talk about that you want to hear about or hear more about:

_____

_____

One key suggestion for improvement: _____

_____

Name of reviewer: _____

Resource O

Preparing a Newscast

Name: _____ Date: _____

Title of report: _____

The event: _____

Who was there? _____

What happened? _____

When did it happen? _____

Where did it happen? _____

Why did it happen? _____

Firsthand account of what you or witnesses saw: Can include quotes

First, _____

Next, _____

Then, _____

Finally, _____

Conclusion (reflect on the event): Thoughts, feelings, reactions, future action

_____

_____

Resource P

Preparing My Position

Name:_____ Date:_____

Argument	Opinions/Reasons

Addressing the Audience

Name: _____   Date: _____

Addressing the Audience

Reason/Argument	Counterargument	Evidence

Resource R

Defending Your Argument

Name: _____   Date: _____

Defending Your Argument

Pros (in favor of your argument/position)	Cons (against your argument/position)
1. _____ Support/evidence: _____ _____ _____	1. _____ Support/evidence: _____ _____ _____
2. _____ Support/evidence: _____ _____ _____	2. _____ Support/evidence: _____ _____ _____
3. _____ Support/evidence: _____ _____ _____	3. _____ Support/evidence: _____ _____ _____
4. _____ Support/evidence: _____ _____ _____	4. _____ Support/evidence: _____ _____ _____

Resource S

Planning for Persuasive Writing

Name: _____   Date: _____

Argument/position: _____

Audience: _____

Opening statement: _____

_____

Thesis: _____

Three reasons: _____

_____

_____

Concluding statement: _____

_____

Opening statement about reason #1: _____

_____

Supporting details:

1. _____

2. _____

3. _____

Counterargument(s): _____

Concluding statement with transition: _____

_____

(Continued)

(Continued)

Opening statement about reason #2: _____

_____

Supporting details:

1. _____

2. _____

3. _____

Counterargument(s): _____

Concluding statement with transition: _____

_____

Opening statement about reason #3: _____

_____

Supporting details:

1. _____

2. _____

3. _____

Counterargument(s): _____

Concluding statement with transition: _____

_____

Restate thesis: _____

_____

Restate three reasons: _____

_____

Concluding statement: _____

_____

Resource T

Persuasive Writing Transition Words

Persuasive Transition Words	Persuasive Transition Words
Add a point	**Add a point**
Again	Again
Also	Also
Although	Although
As well as	As well as
But ... then	But ... then
Equally important	Equally important
Repeatedly	Repeatedly
Yet	Yet
Emphasize or intensify	**Emphasize or intensify**
Above all	Above all
Absolutely	Absolutely
Certainly	Certainly
Even more important	Even more important
Especially	Especially
More important	More important
Obviously	Obviously
Primarily	Primarily
Surely	Surely
Without fail	Without fail
Provide an example	**Provide an example**
For example	For example
In this case	In this case
In this instance	In this instance
To clarify	To clarify
To demonstrate	To demonstrate

Resource U

Peer Revision Sheet for Persuasive Writing

Name of the writer: _____

Thesis/argument: _____

Three main points of the argument:

     1. _____

     2. _____

     3. _____

Is there evidence of the following (check all that apply to their writing)?

Three main points of the argument clearly stated in the introduction: ☐

Persuasive "transition words" are used to give power to the argument: ☐

Opposing viewpoints/perspectives were discussed: ☐

Is each supporting paragraph supported with enough information to give strength to the thesis? ☐

    • If not, what suggestions would you make? _____

    _____

Anything your partner didn't talk about that you want to hear about or hear more about:

_____

_____

One key suggestion for improvement: _____

Name of reviewer: _____

Resource V

Text Support

Name: _____   Date: _____

Text Support

Thesis: _____

Main idea #1: _____

Page	Fact/Example/Quote	Notes

(Continued)

(Continued)

Main idea #2: _____

Page	Fact/Example/Quote	Notes

Main idea #2: _____

Page	Fact/Example/Quote	Notes

Resource W

Planning a Literary Essay

Name: _____ Date: _____

Outline

Book title: _____

Synopsis of the book: _____

_____

_____

_____

Thesis: _____

Main idea #1: _____

Text support: _____

Text support: _____

Connection to thesis: _____

Main idea #2: _____

Text support: _____

Text support: _____

Connection to thesis: _____

Main idea #3: _____

Text support: _____

Text support: _____

Connection to thesis: _____

Resource X

Diamante

Name: _____   Date: _____

Title _____

_____
(noun)

_____ , _____
(adjective)   (adjective)

_____ , _____ , _____
(gerund)   (gerund)   (gerund)

_____ , _____ , _____ , _____
(noun about line 1)   (noun about line 1)   (noun about line 7)   (noun about line7)

_____ , _____ , _____
(gerund for line 7)   (gerund for line 7)   (gerund for line 7)

_____ , _____
(adjective for line 7)   (adjective for line 7)

_____
(noun—opposite line 1)

References

Angelillo, J. (2002). *A fresh approach to teaching punctuation.* Portsmouth, NH: Heinemann.

Adler, D. (2001). *Lou Gehrig: The luckiest man.* Orlando, FL: Harcourt Children's Books.

Allen, J. (2000). *Yellow brick roads: Shared and guided paths to independent reading 4–12.* Portland, MN: Stenhouse Publishers.

Atwell, N. (2002). *Lessons that change writers.* Portsmouth, NH: Heinemann.

Carlson, L. M. (Ed.). (1995). *Cool salsa.* New York: Fawcett by Random House Publishing Group.

Carlson, L. M. (2005). *Red hot salsa: Bilingual poems on being young and latino in the United States.* New York: Macmillan.

Chen, L., & Mora-Flores, E. (2006). *Balanced literacy for English language learners (K-2).* Portsmouth, NH: Heinemann.

Chomsky, N. (1972). *Language and mind.* New York: Harcourt Brace Jovanovich.

Collier, V. P. (1987). Age and rate of acquisition of a second language for academic purposes. *TESOL Quarterly, 21*(4), 617–641.

Collier, V. P., & Thomas, W. P. (2002). *Acquisition of cognitive-academic second language proficiency: A six-year study.* Paper presented at the American Education Research Association conference, New Orleans, LA.

Cummins, J. (1984). Wanted: A theoretical framework for relating language proficiency to academic achievement among bilingual students. In C. Rivera (Ed.), *Language proficiency and academic achievement* (pp. 71–76). Avon, England: Multilingual Matters.

Davies-Samway, K. (2006). *When English language learners write.* Portsmouth, NH: Heinemann.

Fletcher, R. J., & Portalupi, J. (2001). *Writing workshop: The essential guide.* Portsmouth, NH: Heinemann.

Funke, C. (2003). *The thief lord.* New York: Scholastic.

Gibbons, P. (1991). *Learning to learn in a second language.* Portsmouth, NH: Heinemann.

Graham, S., & Harris K. R. (1997). Self-regulation and writing: Where do we go from here? In S. Graham, C. MacArthur, & J. Fitzgerald (Eds.), *Best practices in writing instruction* (pp. 119–140). New York: Guilford Press.

Graham, S., & Harris K. R. (2007). Best practices in teaching planning. In S. Graham, C. MacArthur, & J. Fitzgerald (Eds.), *Best practices in writing instruction* (pp. 119–140). New York: Guilford Press.

Hancock, M. R. (2003). *Celebration of literature and response: Children, books and teachers in K-8 classrooms* (2nd ed.). Upper Saddle River, NJ: Pearson-Prentice Hall.

Harvey, S. (1998). *Non-fiction matters: Reading writing and research in grades 3–8.* Portland, MN: Stenhouse Publishers.

Heard, G. (1998). *Awakening the heart: Exploring poetry in elementary and middle school.* Portsmouth, NH: Heinemann.

Heard, G. (2002). *The revision toolbox: Teaching techniques that work.* Portsmouth, NH: Heinemann.

Kempf, F. R. (1995). The dialectic of education: Foreign language, culture, and literature. *ADFL Bulletin, 27*(1), 38–46.

Krashen, S. D. (1981). *Principles and practice in second language acquisition.* English Language Teaching series. London: Prentice-Hall International.

Krashen, S. D. (2004). *Free voluntary reading: New research, applications, and controversies.* Retrieved February 15, 2007, from http://www.sdkrashen.com/articles/pac5/all.html

Krull, K. (2003). *Harvesting hope: The story of Cesar Chavez.* San Diego, CA: Harcourt Children's Books.

Kucer, S. B. (2005). *Dimensions of literacy: A conceptual base for teaching reading and writing in school settings* (2nd ed.). Mahwah, NJ: Lawrence Erlbaum Associates.

McCormick-Calkins, L. (1994). *The art of teaching writing.* Portsmouth, NH: Heinemann.

Writing Study Group of the National Council of Teachers of English (NCTE) Executive Committee (2004, November). *NCTE beliefs about the teaching of writing.* Retrieved April 30, 2007, from http://www.ncte.org/about/over/positions/category/write/118876.htm

Padgett, R. (2000). *The teachers and writers handbook of poetic forms* (2nd ed.). New York: Teachers and Writers Collaborative.

Peitzman, F. (1992). Coaching the developing second language writer. In P. A. Richard-Amato & M. A. Snow (Eds.), *The multicultural classroom: Readings for content-area teachers* (pp. 198–209). Boston: Addison-Wesley.

Piaget, J. (1983). Piaget's theory. In P. Mussen (Ed.), *Handbook of child psychology* (4th ed.). New York: Wiley.

Pitts, L., Jr. (2000, September 16). Illiteracy is what really scares me. *The Miami Herald,* p. IE.

Pressley, M., Mohan, L., Fingeret, L., Reffitt, K., & Raphael-Bogaert, L. (2007). Writing instruction in engaging and effective elementary settings. In S. Graham, C. MacArthur, & J. Fitzgerald (Eds.), *Best practices in writing instruction* (pp. 13–27). New York: Guilford Press.

Showers, P. (1993). *The listening walk.* New York: HarperCollins Children's Books.

Soto, G. (2000). *Baseball in April and other stories.* Orlando, FL: Harcourt.

Stanovich, K. (1986). Matthew effect in reading: Some consequences of individuals' differences in the acquisition of literacy. *Reading Research Quarterly, 21*(4), 360–407.

Teague, M. (1997). *How I spent my summer vacation.* New York: Crown Publishing Company.

Viorst, J. (1993). *Earrings!* New York: Simon & Schuster Children's Publishing.

Vygotsky, L. (1962). *Thought and language.* Cambridge, MA: MIT Press.

Wood-Ray, K. (1999). *Wondrous words: Writers and writing in the elementary classroom.* Urbana, IL: National Council of Teachers of English.

Index

CORWIN PRESS

The Corwin Press logo—a raven striding across an open book—represents the union of courage and learning. Corwin Press is committed to improving education for all learners by publishing books and other professional development resources for those serving the field of PreK–12 education. By providing practical, hands-on materials, Corwin Press continues to carry out the promise of its motto: **"Helping Educators Do Their Work Better."**